GROWING EVERYDAY DISCIPLES

GROWING EVERYDAY DISCIPLES

COVENANT DISCIPLESHIP WITH CHILDREN

MELANIE C. GORDON
SUSAN GROSECLOSE
GAYLE QUAY

DISCIPLESHIP
RESOURCES

ISBNs
978-0-88177-695-9 (print)
978-0-88177-696-6 (mobi)
978-0-88177-697-3 (ePub)

Library of Congress Control Number: 2016950117

DR695

CONTENTS

INTRODUCTION

Children Are People of the Story

Jesus and the Disciples

Imagine Jesus and the disciples gathered under a tree or by the river, discussing the work of the day. Do you remember how Jesus questioned the disciples in their judgment of others, yet never turned away from them? Instead Jesus used story and experience to teach his disciples how they were to live, loving God and loving their neighbors. Do you remember the question from a lawyer in the crowd, "Who is my neighbor"? (Luke 10:29). We still struggle with understanding who this neighbor is that we are to love. Is it the person living next door? Does it extend to people throughout the community? What about those living on the other side of the world? Jesus describes our neighbor as one who extends mercy to another. Sometimes we ask ourselves, how can I love all these people? I am just one person! That becomes one of the important aspects of Covenant Discipleship. We are in a community with others that allows us to extend the reach of God's love through our actions as a community of disciples. It is true that we can physically touch only those who are living around us, but that does not mean we cannot positively affect the lives of people around the world.

One special characteristic of children is their deep ability to love unconditionally. They come to us primed and ready to love, and we must do all we can to help them express that love by providing them a nurturing environment that helps them grow in the love of Christ. Through our baptismal covenant, we are initiated into the Christian life, and while all the children who participate in Covenant Discipleship may not be baptized, it is through our baptism that we were adopted into the family of God, marking us as disciples of Jesus Christ who show the love of God through works of mercy and piety.

Covenant Discipleship with Children is rooted in Jesus' relationship with the disciples. Jesus and his disciples met as a small group. They prayed together. They worshiped in the company of all who gathered to experience Jesus. Although the disciples sometimes struggled with justice issues, Jesus set the standard as he spoke for those who were oppressed. The Gospels include numerous examples of compassion. We may not possess the gift of healing as Jesus healed, but we are given the gift of compassion, and through compassion, others are healed.

The Holy Club

Imagine a gathered group of young students that included John and Charles Wesley meeting together regularly to study the Bible and the writings of the church. These young men found their small group leading them to serve the poor and the sick and to hold one another accountable for living into the ordinances of the church. Searching the scriptures and meeting together regularly led them to follow a way of life balanced by works of charity throughout the community. This behavior went against the common behavior of the time, and the group was ridiculed by other students. One of the many names they were called stuck—Methodists! We recognize John Wesley as the leader of the Methodist movement and Charles Wesley as the writer of hundreds of hymns of the church.

Years later, the class meeting became a weekly time of prayer, hymn singing, Bible study, and accountability. In class meetings early Methodists learned Christian faith and received the support they needed to live out their faith in daily life. The rule of life for Methodist societies and classes consisted of the General Rules of the Methodist Church, which provided a path for their life in community and in the world as disciples of Jesus Christ. To continue as active members, members were expected to follow the simple rules:

First: By doing no harm, by avoiding evil of every kind, especially that which is most generally practiced.

Secondly: By doing good; by being in every kind merciful after their power; as they have opportunity, doing good of every possible sort, and, as far as possible, to all men . . .

Thirdly: By attending upon all the ordinances [laws and rules] of God. (*The Book of Discipline of The United Methodist Church 2012*)

Covenant Discipleship with Children is a contemporary adaptation of the early Methodist class meeting, guided by the General Rule of Discipleship: "to witness to Jesus Christ in the world and to follow his teachings through acts of compassion, justice, worship, and devotion under the guidance of the Holy Spirit," an understanding of the General Rules used by societies and classes.

> LEARN MORE about the General Rules of The United Methodist Church. See http://www.umc.org/what-we-believe/general-rules-of-the-methodist-church.

Our Children—The Inheritors of the Story

Our children are the inheritors of this rich experience of discipleship, and we promise through our baptismal covenant that we will guide them on the path of true discipleship as we acknowledge in the gathered community to surround them "with a community of love and forgiveness, that they may grow in trust of God, and be found faithful in service to others. We will pray for them, that they may be true disciples who walk in the way that leads to life" ("Baptismal Covenant I," The United Methodist Church, 2009). The way of discipleship requires that we balance our lives and help our children balance their lives through works of mercy and piety. They do not do this on their own. They are born with an innate sense of wonder and a genuine faith in God and depend on parents, caregivers, and responsible adults for every aspect of their care. They are then adopted into God's family, marked as disciples of Jesus Christ, and it is our responsibility to offer them every possible opportunity to live into this covenant so that one day they are fully equipped to make the decision to become professing members of The United Methodist Church.

Our children are blessed with the opportunity to live out the church's story by gathering on a regular basis to strengthen one another as disciples who make disciples. Sarah, who was eleven when asked about her experience in a Covenant Discipleship group, shared that she discovered the needs of people living in her community: "Before Covenant Discipleship group I just saw where I live as a wealthy city; this group has helped me see past that and to see the path of God." If our faith is to live on, our children need to be immersed in holy living—what it means to live as disciples of Jesus Christ. Imagine offering our children personal time of devotion with God, time to worship in the gathered community, time to learn about and respond to justice issues in the world, and time to offer compassion to someone who is hurting. Offering our children this time allows them to grow deeper in their love of God and love of neighbor that will transform our world in ways we have yet to imagine.

> LEARN MORE about baptism: *Baptism— Understanding God's Gift* by L. Edward Phillips and Sara Webb Phillips.

The General Rule of Discipleship

> To witness to Jesus Christ in the world and to follow his teachings through acts of compassion, justice, worship, and devotion under the guidance of the Holy Spirit.
> —*The Book of Discipline of The United Methodist Church 2012*

Again, imagine being present among the people gathered to hear Jesus preach. Imagine a legal expert speaking up and asking Jesus the most important of all the commandments. Do you wonder if this man and the Pharisees expected this response? *"You must love the Lord your God with all your heart, with all your being, and with all your mind. This is the first and the greatest commandment. And the second is like it: You must love your neighbor as you love yourself.* All the Law and the Prophets depend on these two commands" (Matt. 22.37-40, CEB).

The Law and the Prophets depend on these commandments, as does the essence of Covenant Discipleship, which offers us the opportunity to grow deeper in our love of God and neighbor through works of piety and mercy.

Practicing this in life with the love and support of the members of the group, we grow in faith and are led to

- grow deeper in love of God and neighbor;
- understand and live into the connection of loving God and neighbor;
- speak with experience and authority to be disciples making disciples; and
- develop meaningful relationships with the least of these.

As we accept God's grace and steadfast love in our lives, our desire to respond to God's love by loving others grows deeper, equipping us as disciples who make disciples. Covenant Discipleship with Children is a ministry for children who desire to grow deeper in their relationship with Jesus Christ and with others. Through Covenant Discipleship groups, children along with adult guides learn to intentionally and consistently grow in love of God and share God's love with others.

> LEARN MORE about the historical foundations of Covenant Discipleship. See *Accountable Discipleship: Living in God's Household* by Steven Manskar (Discipleship Resources, 2003).

Based on John Wesley's class meetings, Covenant Discipleship challenges children and adult guides to grow as Christian disciples in their daily practice of

- acts of compassion: loving others by helping family members, visiting older adults who are shut in, and other acts of compassion;
- acts of justice: serving in our world by learning about a justice issue in the community, attending a peaceful protest, and other acts of justice;
- acts of worship: praising God through attending worship services, serving as an acolyte, singing in the choir, and other acts of worship;
- acts of devotion: listening and relating to God through prayer, reading the Bible, journaling, and other acts of devotion.

Children and adult guides practice their faith each week through holy living, leading a life of intentional relationship with God while modeling Jesus' life by caring and serving others.

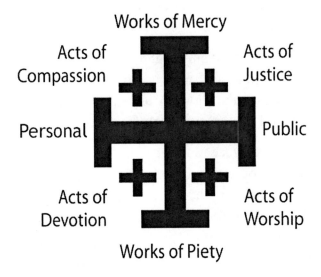

Works of Mercy

Acts of Compassion

Acts of Justice

Personal

Public

Acts of Devotion

Acts of Worship

Works of Piety

This resource is intended for adult guides of children who are committed to helping them grow as disciples of Jesus. You might be a children's minister, a Sunday school teacher, or a pastor who will lead the effort in your congregation; or you may be a parent who will be serving as a guide. As you learn about Covenant Discipleship with Children and consider possibilities for your congregation; be sure to look as well at the book for adults, *Disciples Making Disciples: A Guide for Covenant Discipleship Groups and Class Leaders* by Steven W. Manskar, and the resource for youth, *Everyday Disciples: Covenant Discipleship with Youth* by Chris Wilterdink.

May God bless you and keep you as you serve in Covenant Discipleship with Children.

The Principles of Covenant Discipleship with Children

Therefore, go and make disciples of all nations, baptizing them in the name of the Father and of the Son and of the Holy Spirit, teaching them to obey everything that I've commanded you. Look, I myself will be with you every day until the end of this present age.

—Matthew 28:19-20, CEB

Out of the Great Commission from Matthew 28, quoted above, comes the mission of The United Methodist Church, which is to "make disciples of Jesus Christ for the transformation of the world." Covenant Discipleship with Children is an intentional way for children and guides to live as disciples of Jesus Christ, therefore transforming their lives and the lives of others. Children grow deeper in their relationship with Jesus Christ and others by practicing and living out their discipleship. Through the formational practice of Covenant Discipleship, children live out their faith with acts of compassion, justice, worship, and devotion that allow them to grow in their relationship with God, develop relationships with others in their communities, and transform their lives and the lives of others. In this process, the adult guide serves as an active participant in keeping the group covenant, so he or she forms a deep relationship with the children that rarely occurs in other church settings. The adult becomes both a model and a fellow pilgrim in this Christian journey.

What Is Covenant Discipleship with Children?

Covenant Discipleship is a disciple-shaping process that offers children the opportunity to use their experiences in school, in church, at home, and in the community, discovering ways to "love God and neighbor" through specific acts. Covenant Discipleship forms a rule of life for all of us, especially for our children. The best definition of a rule of life comes from Marjorie Thompson, author of *Soul Feast*: "A rule of life is a pattern of spiritual disciplines that provides structure and direction for growth in holiness. . . . It fosters gifts of the Spirit in personal life and human community, helping to form us into the persons God intends us to be" (Westminster John Knox, 1995, p. 138).

Covenant Discipleship with Children is a specialized ministry for older-elementary-age children who are *ready* to make a commitment to participate and who desire to grow in their discipleship. By participating in a Covenant Discipleship group, children and guides develop a lifelong habit of holy living. This "rule of life" creates a balanced understanding of a life of Christian discipleship expressed through works of piety (loving God) and works of mercy (loving neighbor). John Wesley described works of piety as acts of worship and devotion, and works of mercy as acts of justice and compassion. The works of mercy and the works of piety both have both public and private dimensions. The Jerusalem cross offers a visual image of this balanced practice of discipleship.

Acts of compassion are personal actions of loving others, acts of kindness such as helping family members and visiting older adults who are shut in.

Acts of justice are public actions of serving in our world by joining with others to learn about the causes of a justice issue in the community and taking action to address them.

Acts of worship are public actions that focus on loving God, such as praising God through attending worship services, serving as an acolyte, and singing in the choir.

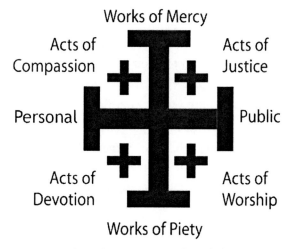

Works of Mercy, Works of Piety

Acts of devotion are private actions focused on loving God, such as listening and relating to God through prayer, reading the Bible, and journaling.

More detailed examples of these acts can be found in the Appendix.

What Do Children's Covenant Discipleship Groups Look Like?

Children's Covenant Discipleship groups are effective with third through sixth graders who are cognitively and emotionally ready to engage in a small group setting that focuses on works of piety and mercy and depends on members' commitment and accountability. In small congregations, there may be one Covenant Discipleship group, while in medium to large congregations, there may be multiple groups.

Each week the children meet for two to two-and-a-half hours. For the first half of their time together, they meet in smaller groups of six to eight children. These are the children's Covenant Discipleship groups, which are led by at least two appointed adult guides. For the second half of their gathering time the Covenant Discipleship groups come together for Justice and Compassion Time, with two or more guides. Other adults participate as speakers, but it is important that only appointed guides and the children meet together during the compassion piece to live more deeply into the covenant.

Outline of a Covenant Discipleship Gathering

Gathering Time: As the children arrive, adult guides offer them a healthy snack and water. The children may go to their group or visit with a friend in another group.

Covenant Time: After ten minutes an adult guide calls the children together with a clap or song and invites them to get settled into their seats. The guides welcome the children and lead them in prayer. Next the group sings two songs, both adult- and child-led.

Guides share goals for the time. Then the larger group breaks into smaller groups for Covenant Sharing.

- They read the covenant together aloud.
- They tell about the acts of compassion, justice, worship, and devotion that members have practiced in the past week.
- They read a selected scripture and discuss it together.
- Guides introduce the justice and compassion activity, which they will participate in during Justice and Compassion Time, and how it connects with the scripture.

Justice and Compassion Time: During the second part of Covenant Discipleship Groups, all the children come together with their adult guides along with special speakers and presenters to carry out the acts of justice and compassion that guides have planned. While Acts of Compassion are personal, it is helpful for children to practice this in groups to strengthen their ability to do this on their own. (Examples are listed previously in the Acts of Compassion and Acts of Justice sections.) This time is spent *going out into the community* to work for justice, to offer compassion or participate in an interactive activity on a justice issue. Children practice being disciples of Jesus Christ and discover ways to show justice and compassion.

Following Justice/Compassion Time, each Covenant Discipleship group gathers briefly for reflection and prayer. Be intentional. This is an important part of the process.

Who Is the Child of the Covenant?

Living into the Great Commandment to love God and neighbor is of course what we want for our children. We offer this way of living as a part of the baptismal covenant we share with Christians around the world. However, there are children who indicate to us that they are ready to go deeper in their relationship with God. These children ask the thought-provoking questions about God and creation, offer to serve others, show a natural empathetic heart, or show other signs of desiring to share their love of God with others. They show an ability to commit to a project. These are children who are *ready* to discover and experience what it means to make a lifelong commitment to Jesus Christ as a professing member of the church. Look for readiness. Remember that this is a transformational experience, and transformation occurs over time.

> To discover more about readiness, download *What Every Child Should Experience: A Guide for Leaders and Teachers in United Methodist Congregations*, developed by Melanie C. Gordon, at umcdiscipleship.org.

Like all children, children of the covenant are formed through relationships and experiences. Covenant Discipleship groups allow children to discover and experience what it means to make a lifelong commitment to Jesus Christ as a professing member of the church. Their adult guides intentionally connect the work of Covenant Discipleship to the vows of membership—prayer, presence, gifts, service, and witness. Children make a connection between the covenant activities and a lifelong commitment as a professing member of God's church.

It is important for adult guides to make every effort to ensure that each child experiences a sense of belonging and acceptance in the group. Many children whom we serve have special needs, and although children in the same age group share developmental similarities, their abilities will vary. Make accommodations for children with physical, cognitive, or behavioral disabilities by talking with parents and church staff to determine the best way to adapt Covenant Discipleship experiences. With the permission of the parents, consider talking to the classroom teacher about accommodations. Identify an adult mentor to assist the children as needed, and consider pairing the child with a sensitive, caring friend in the group. Changing or adapting particular activities will ensure that the children feel included and secure. Medical issues, food allergies and sensitivities, and environmental sensitivities are real and must be accommodated. Prepare and plan accordingly, making every effort to not make accommodations a big deal, as this makes children feel excluded. Through intentional preparations, you offer children hospitality and a sense of belonging.

Children of the covenant must be available to attend the weekly sessions and to commit to following the group covenant. Children, along with their parents or guardians, will need to decide if they can commit to fully participate in a Covenant Discipleship group, especially when they are committed to other extracurricular activities. Children become part of a group that must keep confidentiality; they commit to be faithful to a weekly covenant and to participate in weekly Justice and Compassion Time experiences. Because of this, friends cannot be invited to participate. Children are welcome to invite their friends to talk with the person coordinating Covenant Discipleship to inquire about when a new group will begin. Although children you see in worship and in various ministries of the church will be the first children you consider for Covenant Discipleship with Children, remember to reach out to children of families who are church members but not currently active and children who attend special programs or ministries of the church but are not members.

A powerful example of the transformational power of Covenant Discipleship Groups comes out of a congregation in Oak Ridge, Tennessee. At First United Methodist Church, the congregation committed itself to incorporating small group ministry into the life of the church. In 2006, they began a church-wide Lenten study within these small groups made up of homogeneous groups including older adults, parents of teenagers, and older children.

One of the children's groups consisted of fifth grade girls who wrote their covenant to include means of grace like forgiveness, praying for one another and keeping prayer journals, learning about the mission of church, loving God and neighbor, and extending kindness to others. Sheila Michel, coordinator of small groups at First UMC, witnessed this small group of girls grow from "Prayer Friends" to eighth graders who continue to meet weekly, hold each other accountable, and keep covenant with one another.

When one member of the group noticed that a girl their age was sitting alone outside her little brother's boy scout meeting week after week, she talked to her covenant discipleship group about inviting her to join them. They discussed it and welcomed her. When it became necessary to look at and revise their covenant, they dedicated time to its revision. When one of the members of the group became the target of a bully at school, the group became a place for comfort, support, prayer, and action. Children continue to grow in discipleship through these groups.

Who Are the Adult Guides?

Adults who guide and facilitate Covenant Discipleship with Children groups also live out the group covenant by growing in their own faith. One guide, Lisa, said, "I want to make a difference in my life and in the lives of others."

The coordinator and the adult guides for Covenant Discipleship with Children should possess the following gifts, abilities, and willingness:

- Organizational skills
- Commitment to studying the scriptures
- Regular practice of spiritual disciplines
- An open-minded approach to ministry
- Mission-mindedness
- The gift of working with older elementary children
- A commitment to growing as disciples
- A commitment to the faith formation of children and families
- Active membership in a Covenant Discipleship group
- Solid communication skills:
- Observation skills
- Ongoing Safe Sanctuaries® training

As one guide, Rory, said, "I find that I have grown spiritually myself by being in relationship with the children and other adult guides. After all, as one of my former colleagues used to say, 'You can't go on teaching if you don't go on learning.'"

Coordinators of Covenant Discipleship with Children have the responsibility to plan, implement, and evaluate this ministry and are expected to

- read and become familiar with this Covenant Discipleship resource;
- inform and educate congregational leaders about Covenant Discipleship with Children;
- plan logistics, budget, and publicity;
- recruit and train guides;
- plan Justice and Compassion Time with group guides that include identifying the justice and compassion focus, plan logistics for the children's education and response, and prepare supplies, resources, speakers, and visits needed;
- offer ongoing information for parents and children interested in participating;
- provide general oversight of the Covenant Discipleship groups;
- provide resources and supplies to group guides;
- arrange a service of dedication for Covenant Discipleship groups (see page 36);
- keep the congregation informed about Covenant Discipleship with Children and ways the ministry is forming children as disciples and transforming the community;
- continue to recruit and train new adult guides;
- meet with new parents and children who might be interested in participating; and
- initiate formal and informal evaluations for future planning.

Each Adult Guide of Covenant Discipleship with Children has the responsibility to

- read and become familiar with this Covenant Discipleship resource;
- prepare for and be present for group gatherings and outings
- support the coordinator in planning Justice and Compassion Time that includes identifying the justice and compassion focus, planning logistics for the children's education and response, and preparing supplies, resources, speakers, and visits;

- offer ongoing information for parents and children interested in participating;
- assist the coordinator in keeping the congregation informed about Covenant Discipleship with Children and ways the ministry is forming children as disciples and transforming the community; and
- help identify children to participate in Covenant Discipleship with Children groups.

There is no question that Covenant Discipleship with Children groups transform the lives of children, adult guides, presenters, parents, and families. Through participation in these particular small groups, transformation happens in the congregation and the community. One amazing example can be found at Buncombe Street United Methodist Church in Greenville, South Carolina. Covenant Discipleship groups with children have been active in this church for years. The congregation sees the children each week in their "Sprouts" T-shirts serving as greeters at the sanctuary doors and nursery helpers. Gayle Quay, the Covenant Discipleship coordinator, provides numerous opportunities for the congregation to read about the justice projects the children are involved in, support the children on walks for the hungry and homeless, and even occasionally join the children in mission projects. This congregation realizes how the children and their guides are touching the lives of the community and beyond. The children are known throughout the Greenville community and have received numerous recognitions for their work. However, Gayle reports that "the biggest impact on the community is seeing in the eyes of the homeless, drug addicts, recovering drug addicts, hungry children and families, and agency employees that older-elementary children care and want to make a difference!" (For more about the children's experiences with Covenant Discipleship, see "The Story of Covenant Discipleship with Children at Buncombe Street United Methodist Church, page 52.)

> LEARN MORE about planning. See *Guidelines for Leading Your Congregation* by Melanie C. Gordon. (Cokesbury.com)

Planning Covenant Discipleship with Children

Planning Covenant Discipleship groups that will be transformational requires intentionality. After reading this resource, communicating with all of those who will be involved is your first step. This will help you to determine schedules, leadership, and logistics needed for this ministry. This is also a good time to gauge the role that Covenant Discipleship can play in preparing children for confirmation.

Communicating with Parents and Guardians

Parents want to be kept informed and included. E-mail or text a weekly note and a monthly calendar or a newsletter to share stories and announce upcoming Justice and Compassion Time experiences. A few weeks after the Covenant Discipleship groups begin, contact parents again to get feedback about strengths and challenges they are seeing. Remind them about ways they can be helpful to their children.

- Regular attendance is important.
- Discussions between the children and their guides are confidential.

- Guides depend on parents and other responsible adults to encourage their children to live out their covenant through acts of devotion, worship, compassion, and justice.
- Guides are always available for children or their parents.

Communicating with Adult Guides

Check with guides on a regular basis for feedback.

- Ask about additional information, ideas, supplies, or resources they need.
- Show appreciation for their ministry and offer encouragement.
- Assure guides that you are available if a particular concern arises with a child or a Covenant Discipleship group.

Communicating with the Congregation, District, and Annual Conference

Keep the congregation informed about how children are growing as disciples of Jesus Christ through Covenant Discipleship with Children.

- Invite children and guides to share how the Covenant Discipleship group is making a difference in their lives. Share these stories and comments in the church e-newsletter, on the church website, or through social media.
- Take photographs of the groups and post them on the church's website or on a bulletin board. Sharing photographs publicly is a privacy issue and we want to protect our children. Refer to the congregation's Safe Sanctuaries® Media Policy for guidance and permissions.
- Invite the congregation to participate in an act of justice along with the children and guides.
- Publish letters from government or community guides regarding the results of the children's acts of justice.
- Incorporate prayers written by the children in the worship liturgy.
- Continue to encourage children and worship leadership to include children in leading worship.
- Children who are willing may talk about their experiences to other small groups in the congregation.

- Staff a booth at an annual conference meeting. This could be done at a district or conference training event for children's ministry leaders. Arrange for the children to wear their identifiers and to share their stories and pictures.

When Will Covenant Discipleship Groups Gather?

Consider the schedules of the children whom you are inviting to participate. While you know that it is impossible to plan the perfect schedule, consider the following:

- How many weeks will the Covenant Discipleship groups meet? Some churches have found that it is useful to meet for a specific term of ten to twelve weeks while other churches plan to meet for a school-year term or a portion of the school year.
- How long will each weekly session last? You need to plan for at least ninety minutes, but if the group will be traveling for many of the Justice and Compassion Time experiences, or if you are including a snack or light meal, you may choose to meet for two to two-and-a-half hours.

Once a decision has been made as to the day of the week and the time of day, remember to add the dates to the church calendar. At the end of each term, review the schedule. Will a change make participation easier for children? For their parents? For the adult guides? Will a change in the schedule make it possible for more children to participate? Always be open to making adjustments as they are needed.

Where Will Covenant Discipleship Groups Gather?

You will need a gathering space large enough for all the children to gather at one time. You will also need rooms for children to comfortably break out for Covenant Sharing. Each Covenant Discipleship group will need its own room to share with one another and where the group can maintain confidentiality. Provide a table and chairs as well as basic supplies such as paper, pencils, Bibles, and hymnals so that children can work on Bible activities, write or draw their prayers, write or draw in their journals, and pray together. Consider including a worship area with Christian Year seasonal cloth, cross, candle, or other worship items in each Covenant Sharing room.

Several groups can meet together for Justice and Compassion Time. This room will need to be adequate space for children to move as they view videos, play simulation games, complete art projects, pack care packages, or participate in mission projects. The setup for this room might change depending on the week's activities, but be sure to secure tables, chairs, and a place to store supplies well in advance of Justice and Compassion Time.

The Weekly Schedule

Decide on a weekly schedule that meets the needs of your group. Remember to provide a balance between Covenant Sharing and Justice and Compassion Time. Questions to consider:

- Will Covenant Sharing incorporate Bible reading and reflection, prayer, or other discipleship skills?
- Will most of the Justice and Compassion Time experiences take place at the church or other locations?
- Will you alternate between a week learning and preparing for service in the community and a week serving in the community? Many churches realize the benefit to children when they experience firsthand justice and compassion issues and when they are seen in the community working for justice and offering compassion.

Sample Groupings and Schedules

Schedule A: Total group of up to six children

Gathering Time: 10 minutes

Covenant Time: 45 minutes

- Opening prayer and songs: 15 minutes
- Covenant sharing (stay in one group): 30 minutes

Justice and Compassion Time: 45–60 minutes

Schedule B: Total group of six to ten children

Gathering Time: 10 minutes

Covenant Time: 45 minutes

- Opening prayer and songs: 15 minutes
- Covenant sharing (divide into two groups): 30 minutes

Justice and Compassion Time: 45–60 minutes

Schedule C: Total group of more than ten children

Gathering Time: 10 minutes

Covenant Time: 45 minutes

- Opening prayer and songs: 15 minutes
- Covenant sharing (divide into two or more groups): 30 minutes

Justice and Compassion Time: 45–60 minutes

Planning Snack Time

If you plan to serve a snack or light meal during the sessions, consider the logistical needs for food preparation and eating. Decide who will provide the snack.

Here are some ideas (allergy considerations apply):

- Include snacks in the budget and ask a member of the congregation who is unable to serve as a guide to volunteer to purchase snacks for each week.
- Ask parents to sign up for a week to provide either a simple snack or a light meal.
- Have a snack box (large plastic container). Assign each child a week to provide the snack. Whoever is assigned to bring snacks takes the box home and returns with it full of snacks. Remind the children that sharing food with others is one way of being a faithful disciple.
- Choose snacks that are simple, inexpensive, and nutritious. Fresh fruit and nutrition bars are good choices. Stick to water as the drink of choice. Remind children of the importance of caring for their own bodies.

- Avoid environmentally wasteful packaging such as individually packaged drinks or snacks. Remind the children that we are learning to care for God's creation and the environment.
- When possible, plan snacks relevant to the learning activities.

Developing a Budget

As you prepare your budget for Covenant Discipleship with Children, these questions will be helpful:

- How will you promote the new effort? What are the printing and mailing costs for letters, brochures, and other information? What will you promote on your church's website, blog, or through social media?
- What training expenses for your guides will you incur?
- What books, videos, or resources on compassion, justice, worship, and devotion are available to borrow from your church, conference, or community library? What resources will need to be purchased?
- Will you provide honorariums for Justice and Compassion Time speakers?
- Are there transportation costs? Will children be picked up after school or will parents bring children? What will be your travel expenses to various organizations in the community? Do you have a church van or bus or will you need to recruit volunteers to provide transportation?
- Are basic supplies available or will you need to purchase them? What additional supplies will you need to purchase?
- If you plan to provide a snack or light meal, will this be purchased or will you ask parents to provide food?
- Churches have found it beneficial for children and guides to wear identifiers like T-shirts, visors, or bracelets. This creates a sense of belonging, helps congregational members identify the children when they are serving in the church, and provides a way for the group to be safe when serving in the community. Will the church provide the identifier or will the parents purchase them?
- How much of this ministry will be funded through the church's children's ministry, Christian education, or another ministry budget? If all the expenses are not covered, are there people in the congregation interested

in providing financial support? Will families be asked to pay a nominal fee for their children to participate in the Covenant Discipleship groups? How often will participants be asked to provide items for a particular mission project?

Evaluation

For the ongoing, faithful ministry of Covenant Discipleship with Children it is important to evaluate the program regularly. Evaluation is the tool that will keep the program fresh and relevant for the children and guides who participate.

- Each guide will evaluate each individual session to make decisions about planning for the next session. This can be as informal as a conversation.
- The coordinator, along with the children's minister or children's ministry team, will periodically evaluate the group configurations, schedule, meeting space, and weekly sessions. This evaluation will help plan for the future and determine what additional training and support the coordinator and guides need.
- Children gain a sense of ownership when they are involved in ongoing evaluation and feedback. Give them opportunities to suggest topics for Justice and Compassion Time, to plan ways to announce formation of new groups, and to share with the congregation about their experience in Covenant Discipleship groups.
- Give parents an opportunity to evaluate. Parents may be your best source of information about how Covenant Discipleship groups are affecting the lives of children.
- Both informal and formal evaluations are essential. You can informally ask for feedback from the children, guides, and parents throughout the term.
- Provide an opportunity at the end of each term for a formal evaluation. You can find sample evaluation forms for guides, parents, and children in the appendices and writable PDFs online at http://www.umcdiscipleship. org/CDChildren. The feedback will confirm the importance of this ministry and provide insight for making improvements.

Guiding This Pilgrimage

Faith formation is a lifelong process in which people claim their identity as beloved children of God and their call to participate in God's purposes for the world. This process begins at birth and involves *information* (what we know), *formation* (who we are and who we are becoming), and *transformation* (how the world is changed because of who we are and how we live). A life of faith, then, includes cognitive, emotional, and behavioral dimensions. The effectiveness of this process directly affects how well a local church fulfills its mission "to make disciples of Jesus Christ for the transformation of the world" (*The Book of Discipline of The United Methodist Church 2012*, ¶120).

Recruiting Adult Guides for Covenant Discipleship Groups

As you consider inviting people to serve as guides, a participant in an adult Covenant Discipleship group is ideal. If your church does not have a Covenant Discipleship ministry, consider adults who possess the characteristics of a guide and show interest in caring and nurturing children's faith development. As you choose guides, it is important that they are caring for their own spiritual formation and are interested in nurturing children in their faith development. An effective guide will be a strong role model and mentor for all children, living out their membership vows through their prayers, Bible study, engagement in worship, gifts of time and finances, service to others, and a witness of God's compassion and justice.

The number of adult guides will be determined by two factors: the total number of children you anticipate will participate in the weekly Covenant Discipleship gathering and the number of Covenant Sharing and Justice and Compassion Time groups. Guides must be willing to share responsibility for preparation and facilitation of each week's session and also to fully participate in the Covenant Time and Justice and Compassion Time along with the children.

Covenant Sharing conversation is confidential, so the same guides must be present each week. Adult guides must adhere to the promise to keep confidentiality, balancing this with the importance of protecting children who may be in harmful situations. With this in mind, *do not* allow parents to be guides of Covenant Sharing that includes their own children. Provide a safe environment for children and guides by following the Safe Sanctuaries® guideline of at least two nonrelated, non-cohabitating adults present during the entire Covenant Time. Since, ideally, members in a Covenant Discipleship group develop trust with one another, make every effort to assign three guides to a group so that the group does not experience disruption if a guide must be absent.

Guides of the Justice and Compassion Time may change each week as the topics of discussion and activities change. In addition to the weekly guides, consider inviting other people in the congregation or district or annual conference leaders with specific knowledge or experience in particular areas. Community organization leaders, government officials, doctors, and social workers are also good resources for Justice and Compassion Time.

If transportation is provided for the children, it is important for the drivers to be faithful Christians, trained in Safe Sanctuaries®, and knowledgeable about Covenant Discipleship with Children. They, too, will be role models for the children and will field questions from parents and people in the community.

Training Covenant Discipleship Guides

Once guides are identified, schedule a training session well before the first Covenant Discipleship gathering with the children. If nearby churches are planning to offer Covenant Discipleship groups for children, a joint guide training might be a good idea, particularly if you have only a few guides. Another possibility is to partner with other churches in your area to sponsor a district-wide training for Covenant Discipleship with Children. This training could be for guides of children's Covenant Discipleship groups as well as adults who are interested in beginning Covenant Discipleship with Children in their local congregation. Consider including a time for the guides to plan Covenant Sharing and Justice and Compassion Time during the training. If that is not a possibility, make sure to schedule a special time for this planning.

See "Model for Training for Adult Guides of Children's Covenant Discipleship Groups" (pages 66–77).

Inviting Parents and Guardians into Covenant Discipleship

Like all ministries that involve children, Covenant Discipleship groups with children require commitment from parents and guardians. Parents help children live into the covenant through encouragement and intentional listening.

Invite parents of children in third through sixth grades to an informational meeting to learn about Covenant Discipleship, characteristics of a child of the covenant, commitment to the group and activities, and the transformational impact of participation in a Covenant Discipleship group. Your church may have a system in place for this type of invitation. Here are some additional ways to promote the meeting:

- Use the sample letter and publicity flier provided in this resource (see the appendices). A writable PDF can be found at http://www.umcdiscipleship. org/CDChildren
- Include an announcement in the church e-newsletter, newsletter, or church bulletin.
- Use social media to encourage attendance and involvement.
- Ask the pastor(s) to publicly support Covenant Discipleship with Children groups.
- Visit ministries that include children to generate excitement about this new effort in which they will have an opportunity to put what they are experiencing and learning about Christianity into action.

- Visit ministries that include parents of children and share how their children's spiritual formation will be enhanced through a Covenant Discipleship.
- Ask people who have participated in Covenant Discipleship groups to share their experience during a worship service.
- Mail to parents and guardians an invitation and brochure that briefly describes Covenant Discipleship groups.

See "Model for a Parent and Child Meeting" (pages 63–66).

Assigning Children and Guides to Covenant Discipleship Groups

Once children register and adult guides are trained, assign children and guides to Covenant Discipleship groups, which are primarily covenant sharing groups. As you make assignments, keep these guidelines in mind.

- These groups may be mixed-grade or single-grade groups, single gender or mixed gender, depending on what works best for the number, ages, and needs of the children.
- Try to keep six to eight children in each group and at least two adult guides who can facilitate each week.
- The discussions that take place during Covenant Sharing are confidential and must not be discussed by the children or guides outside this setting. Remind and train guides to follow Safe Sanctuaries® guidelines when the safety and security of a child surfaces in a conversation.
- Several Covenant Discipleship groups can meet together for Justice and Compassion Time.
- Provide a sufficient number of adult guides to plan and carry out the justice and compassion activities. Follow appropriate Safe Sanctuaries® guidelines.
- Outside speakers and leaders such as mission chairpersons or directors of community organizations may be a valuable addition.

Take time to pray about the way groups are assigned. There are two options to consider after prayer. Once you have assigned children and adult guides to a group, you may choose to notify the children, their parents, and the guides.

You may also want to wait and share the assignments at the first gathering. As they begin this pilgrimage of holy living, share dates and times of the Covenant Discipleship gatherings and also the date and time for the service of dedication.

Provide parents and guardians with the following information:

- Group assignments
- Date Covenant Discipleship groups begin
- Room locations
- The first Covenant Discipleship group gathering, calendar of activities, and T-shirts or other identifiers that children will wear when serving in the community

Configuring Groups

As you determine the configuration of the groups, consider the number of children expected to participate, their ages, and the maturity of the children in your congregation. Knowing the children of your congregation is important. Some possible groupings are

- one group for grades 3–6;
- two groups: one for grades 3–4 and another for grades 5–6;
- two groups: one for grades 3–5 and a separate group for grade 6 (which could serve as a pre-confirmation group);
- four groups: a separate group for each grade level; and
- girls in one group and boys in another group.

Consider these or other options that work in your congregation.

If children will be participating more than one year, you might consider a group for first-year Covenant Discipleship participants and another group for second-year participants. As children grow spiritually, it might be useful for the children's covenant and their compassion and justice experiences to be shaped by and build upon the first-year experience. For example, the first year, the children might write in their covenant to pray for their family, while the second year, the children might choose to practice different ways of praying. A group of children in the first year might participate in a community worship service for the homeless, and the second-year children would lead the worship service.

At the end of each year, carefully review the group configurations and make needed adjustments for the next year.

A Service of Dedication for Covenant Discipleship Groups

At the point that you are assigning children and guides to Covenant Discipleship groups, make sure the pastor and worship team are preparing for the service of dedication. The dedication takes place after the group or groups have written their covenant. You will find one available at http://www.umcdiscipleship.org/resources/a-service-of-dedication-for-covenant-discipleship-groups.

Make this litany available for parents and children well in advance so that they may be familiar with the language and their responses. Invite parents and guides to stand with the children and lay hands on them during the service.

Acts of Compassion, Justice, Worship, and Devotion

Compassion

Covenant Discipleship groups for children in your congregation might consider acts of compassion like these:

- Visiting older adults in assisted living, a long-term care facility, or an older adult in the church member's home. The group can make a craft together, visit and share stories, or sing together.
- Collecting canned food, socks and underwear, hats and gloves, or toiletries for a community organization.
- Preparing and serving a meal for the guests at a nearby community agency. Also plan ways for the children to interact with those they are serving.
- Donating new children's books to a shelter for women and children or to families in a low-income area where children do not have adequate access to books.
- Adopting environmental projects. Children can keep a section of a road free of litter, pick up trash around the church, participate in a community shredding event, or another community project.
- Participating in a toy drive. Children can collect and deliver new or gently used toys to an afterschool or child-care program.

- Doing random acts of compassion. Arrange for children to make cookies or brownies or thank-you cards for local police officers, firefighters, hospital staff, or another local service organization.
- Participating in staff appreciation day. Invite children to find ways to show appreciation to your church staff. You might offer to clean the yard of the parsonage, prepare snacks or lunch for the staff, or wash their cars.
- Assembling UMCOR kits (United Methodist Committee on Relief). Help children collect and assemble items for school kits or flood buckets.
- Helping with Stop Hunger Now. Children may participate in local church or community project to package meals for the hungry.
- Filling weekend backpacks. Make arrangements for children to join a community organization to fill backpacks with nonperishable food. These backpacks are given to schools so that children who receive free or reduced school lunches will also have food on the weekends.
- Participating in Make a Difference Day. Involve children in a community-wide day of service. If your community does not have a day of service, plan your own compassion project by organizing one within your congregation. Identify and research the needs of three to four service organizations, making sure you include service projects that families can do together. Decide on a date and time. Promote the day by sharing stories and information about the work of the different organizations. One church offered a simple breakfast and devotion before church members were deployed to their service projects. Other churches have held the day of service on a Sunday and begin with a brief worship service sending members out to work in the community.
- Creating Sacks of Smiles for people who are homeless. Children can fill paper bags with items that can be kept in the car, distributed as a group, or sold to church members to distribute. "Sell" the bags for five dollars to church members before worship. Fill bags with a bottle of water, information on where to get assistance, a card made by the children, a nutrition bar, and toiletry items.

Justice

Covenant Discipleship with Children groups in your congregation might consider acts of justice like these:

- Partnering with community organizations. Learn about organizations within your community and invite a representative to talk with the children. This will allow them to discover justice issues in their community and ways to respond to local justice issues.
- Contacting national and global organizations. Request learning materials and resources that will help children learn about and respond to justice issues. Habitat for Humanity, Heifer International, the Society of St. Andrew, United Methodist Committee on Relief, and One.Org are all good places to start. These resources are readily found online.
- Raising awareness. Create brochures, videos, or other information items to raise awareness of justice issues the group is learning about. Post information in the church's newsletter, on its webpage, or via its social media account.
- Holding prayer vigils. Sponsor a prayer vigil relating to a particular justice issue like the Children's Sabbath (childrensdefense.org; see the "Library" tab) or World AIDS Day.
- Creating bags of blessings. Work with the group to set up a store with school supplies, hats, gloves, toiletries, or other items needed by a community organization. Share information about the organization, the injustice that they are addressing, and stories of the persons they serve. Invite church members to either purchase a bag for ten to fifteen dollars or to shop in the store to fill their own bags. Individuals may choose to purchase a box in honor or memory of someone. The group sends acknowledgments to the family who is being honored or memorialized.
- Writing letters to local news outlets, legislators, church officials, businesses, school board members, or anyone who might have influence on a particular justice issue you are working on.
- Planning a fair trade market. Educate your congregation about alternative forms of giving, like buying fair trade items. ("Fair trade" refers to producers of the goods, often people in developing countries, being treated

ethically and receiving a fair price for their products.) Invite community organizations and companies to provide informational materials, fair trade gifts to purchase, and donation cards. Be sure to provide simple crafts for younger children while parents shop.

- Participating in the Children's Fund for Christian Mission. Plan to participate in this mission sponsored jointly by United Methodist Global Ministries and Discipleship Ministries of The United Methodist Church.
- Planning peaceful protests. Discuss and research a current justice issue, and participate in or plan a peaceful protest.
- Respecting diversity. Be intentional about discussions on equality issues. Offer opportunities for children to learn about discrimination in our society. Let children create an informational presentation with images that include people of different races, genders, nationalities, religions, abilities, ages, and economic conditions to share with The United Methodist Women and adult Sunday school classes or with the congregation during worship.
- Watching for annual peace and justice events on the calendar. Volunteer to organize Peace with Justice Sunday (umcgiving.org).

Worship

Covenant Discipleship with Children groups in your congregation might consider acts of worship like these:

- Singing songs of our faith. Use *The United Methodist Hymnal, The Faith We Sing, The Upper Room Worshipbook, Worship and Song, The Africana Hymnal: Black Sacred Music,* and *Global Praise* to learn and sing songs as you begin weekly meetings, open or close Covenant Time, study a justice issue, travel to a justice or compassion experience, or close a weekly meeting.
- Learning about and participating in the Lord's Supper. Children can study the background and meaning of Holy Communion and assist in serving Communion. Do a short study from *This Holy Mystery—A Study Guide for Children and Youth* by Carolyn Tanner.

- Learning about baptism. Children can study the background and meaning of baptism through *I Belong to God!* by Carolyn Tanner and make cards to welcome the child or adult into God's family.
- Serving at worship. Arrange for the children to serve as ushers or greeters during worship or set up a regular rotation with the worship committee so that two to three children serve each week. They can serve as acolyte, crucifer, liturgist, reader, or sing in the choir.
- Learning about worship. Teach the children about the forms and rituals of the worship service and the seasons of the Christian Year. Use *Come! Come! Everybody Worship* by Carolyn Tanner.
- Visiting other houses of worship. Visit a worship service at a nearby synagogue, mosque, or church of another Christian denomination. Explore the possibility of the children meeting other children in the congregation for a time of fellowship and mutual learning. Lead a conversation on the similarities and differences of the services.
- Participating in a Love Feast. Learn about the history of the Love Feast and let the children plan and lead one. The full service can be found in *The United Methodist Book of Worship* and "A Brief Order of the Love Feast" can be found online at umcdiscipleship.org/worship.

Devotion

Covenant Discipleship with Children groups in your congregation might consider acts of devotion like these:

- Reading a scripture passage together. Ask questions about the passage, helping children make the connection between scripture and how we live our lives. Remember to be sensitive to children who may not feel comfortable reading aloud. The goal is to help children develop Bible reading as a personal act of devotion.
- Reading reflectively. Read a scripture passage to the children. Ask the children to list or draw what they heard, saw, smelled, tasted, and felt as they heard the scripture passage. Let them volunteer to share or display their creations.

- Creating a devotion booklet. Explore the liturgical calendar together. Choose a season and create a devotional booklet to distribute to the congregation.
- Sharing group prayer concerns. Ask the children for prayer requests. They may write their requests on slips of paper and place them in a box in the room. Model writing each prayer concern for the children and encourage them to write the requests so that they can pray for their group concerns during the week. Ask the children about how their prayers have been answered during the previous week. Concentrate specifically on prayer concerns discussed the week before.
- Making prayer requests. Receive your congregation's weekly prayer list and guide children in offering prayers of intercession. If your church does not have an active prayer request ministry, you can start one by providing prayer cards in the worship pews and inviting church members to submit their prayer requests to the children.
- Forming prayer partners. Assign prayer partners within the group.
- Praying prayers from *The United Methodist Hymnal*. Using the index of the hymnal, choose a prayer that corresponds to the season of the year or a specific act of compassion or act of justice.
- Writing creation prayers. Take the group outside and encourage them to write about their natural surroundings. They can create poems, list observations, or draw a picture expressing God's creative power. Children may share the prayers with the group if they choose.

Planning Future Covenant Discipleship Groups

Planning ahead will allow you to reach more children and families in your congregation and in the community.

- As you approach the end of each term, talk with the children, parents, and guides about their participation in the next term.
- Begin publicity and registration for new and returning participants.
- Before the beginning of each new term, send letters to parents of potential new participants and either offer another information session or meet with children and parents one-on-one to provide information.

- Meet with Covenant Discipleship group guides to shape training, explore resources, and plan future Justice and Compassion Time.

Assign responsibilities for contacting guest speakers, arranging field trips, or other organizational responsibilities.

End-of-Term Activity or Event

At the end of the term, you might plan a special closing event to celebrate the children's work and growth in discipleship. This is an excellent time for the children, parents, and guides to reflect and share their experiences.

Many options can offer a lasting impact on children, such as a family event like a picnic, showing a video that highlights the children's experiences, gathering to share stories and sing some favorite songs and hymns, or anything that allows children to bring together their experiences of Covenant Discipleship in community.

"Night in a Box" is a hands-on, overnight experience to culminate a justice issue on homelessness. Provide large cardboard boxes or have each child bring their own box. The children decorate their cardboard box home and find a location inside or outside the church where they will live for the night. Prepare a simple meal similar to the type of meal served at a homeless shelter, or visit a homeless shelter to help prepare and serve a meal. This will also give the children an opportunity to visit with the guests. Take a night walk through your city or town streets where the homeless often live. Invite a person who is homeless or works with the homeless to talk with the children. Be sure that the children have prepared questions beforehand to ask the visitor. During the night, the children sleep in their box wearing only a pair of pants, T-shirt, and shoes. The next morning invite the parents and members of the congregation to join the children for a simple breakfast. Conclude with a time of celebration and a worship experience planned by the children.

Expanding Covenant Discipleship with Children

Now that you have the basics, you can explore ways to enrich and expand the children's experiences. For example, during Covenant Sharing, the purpose is for children and guides to share how they are following the covenant and growing as disciples of Jesus Christ. However, becoming more familiar with their Bible, practicing different forms of prayer, worshiping together, understanding the elements and rituals of worship and the sacraments, or other discipleship skills enrich the children's experience by providing activities for children to practice living out their covenant together. You will find ways for the group to practice acts of devotion and acts of worship together. Visit http://www.umcdiscipleship. org/CDChildren to discover more ideas to stimulate your creativity, and share acts that have worked for your Covenant Discipleship group. *Growing Everyday Disciples* will help children grow as disciples of Jesus Christ who make disciples, deepening their love of God and neighbor as they continue to grow in faith.

Covenant Discipleship as Pre-Confirmation

Children who are preparing to begin confirmation can discover that Covenant Discipleship groups are an excellent way for them to live out their baptismal vows through works of piety and mercy. Covenant Discipleship groups offer children who are walking similar paths of discipleship to meet together for mutual accountability and support. This form of Christian discipleship is deeply rooted in the theology of John Wesley's way of salvation.

> *Prevenient grace* literally means "the grace that comes before." Prevenient grace calls us into a relationship with God before we are even aware of God. It prepares us for the dawning awareness that God loves us so much that God seeks us out first.
>
> *Justifying grace* offers reconciliation, forgiveness of sin, freedom from the power and guilt of sin, and the possibility of new relationships with God and with one another.
>
> *Sanctifying grace* enables us to grow into the image of Christ and to live as a sign of God's reign among us. Sanctifying grace leads to inward and outward holiness. (*Foundations: Shaping the Ministry of Christian Education in Your Congregation*, Discipleship Ministries, 2012; downloadable PDF at http://www.umcdiscipleship.org/resources/foundations)

This Is Your Baptismal Liturgy summarizes confirmation in this way: "God confirms the divine promise to those who were too young to grasp what God was doing in their baptism, they respond by professing their own acceptance of the grace they have received and their own faith in Christ, and the Church, as represented by this congregation, confirms the commitments they make." Time spent in prayer and searching the scriptures, addressing justice issues, serving those in need in the community, regular participation in worship, and meeting for mutual accountability will allow children more intentional time to deeply consider what it means to become a professing member of The United Methodist Church.

Covenant Discipleship helps children and adult guides learn and live this faith and to accept God's good news for themselves. They learn about living as a child of God who is forgiven, loved, and free to become the person God created her or him to be. It offers an intentional way to live as disciples of Jesus Christ growing in their faith and transforming themselves and their relationships with others.

For Rory, a seasoned guide, Covenant Discipleship groups are important because, as he says, "I get to watch the children grow in spiritual, social, and emotional understandings; and I have seen, over my years as a guide, how the experiences of the children have prepared them to participate in confirmation and to join the church as fully participating members."

The First Gathering

And he said to them, "Follow me, and I will make you fish for people."
—Matthew 4:19

The first gathering of Covenant Discipleship groups introduces children and guides to the Covenant Discipleship process. During this time, they will get to know one another, talk about what it means to be a disciple of Jesus Christ, and begin to understand Covenant Time and Justice and Compassion Time. If you have more than one group, during this first gathering, keep all the children and guides together rather than dividing the session into Covenant Time groups and Justice and Compassion Time group(s). Make sure you make allowances for children needing movement and tactile stimulation. This time should be engaging, not simply for lecture.

Prepare the children by letting them know which group they are in and where their group will be meeting the next week. Before the meeting, assign the children to Covenant Discipleship groups of six to eight children with at least two nonrelated, non-cohabitating guides for Covenant Sharing. For larger groups, decide if all the Covenant Discipleship groups will come together for Justice and Compassion Time or if groups will be paired.

A lesson plan for the first gathering is included at the end of this chapter.

Covenant Discipleship Groups and Covenant Sharing Conversations

At the beginning of each week's session, the children and guides meet in small groups for approximately thirty minutes for Covenant Sharing. During this time, the children and guides support and encourage one another in their Christian journey. In the beginning, especially with children unfamiliar with Covenant Discipleship, you will need to spend time teaching about the acts of discipleship and the importance of being faithful to the covenant. A significant portion of the first few Covenant Sharing times will be spent writing the group covenant. Once the covenant is written, most of Covenant Sharing will be spent talking about how the children and guides are following the covenant each week and supporting one another as disciples of Jesus Christ.

Children Experience Covenant Sharing

We all come to faith in different ways and at different times in our lives. The children in Covenant Discipleship groups will have different experiences in their faith journey. As children learn to trust one another and are more open in sharing, expect that the children will ask faith-probing questions, share deeper feelings about their relationship with God and others, and share the joys and struggles they experience in being disciples of Jesus Christ. As you participate in Covenant Sharing with them, these are points to remember:

- Offer unchurched children the same hospitality as churched children.
- Make Bibles available for all children.
- Help children learn significant theological terms.
- Be patient as children grow in understanding the importance of confidentiality.
- Communicate clearly with parents so they understand how to support their children.

Through participation in Covenant Sharing, children will

- develop a sense of belonging, while learning to be inclusive of those who are different;

- learn mutual respect;
- practice forgiveness;
- struggle with difficult moral issues and confront their own prejudices;
- learn to respond to a concern with action that makes a difference;
- stand up for others and dare to be different from their peers; and
- develop skills, sensitivity, and caring necessary for becoming advocates for those who are voiceless or live on the margins of society.

Pockets (http://pockets.upperroom.org/) is a great devotional resource for children to use at home for devotion time. The magazine is published monthly by the Upper Room Ministries, offering children scripture, prayers, stories about children, and examples of ways to offer compassion to others.

Leading Covenant Sharing

Once the group has written their covenant, the children and adults will share each week how they are following the covenant during the week. Guides are key in modeling and teaching children how to support and encourage one another. Consider the following suggestions when leading the Covenant Sharing conversations:

- At the beginning of each Covenant Sharing, read the covenant aloud as a group. Be mindful of reading comfort levels of children.
- Ask each child to describe the acts he or she has lived out in each of the areas—compassion, justice, worship, devotion—during the week.
- The guide holds a key responsibility to follow the covenant in his or her life. The guide models how to offer forgiveness and grace when commitments are unmet and ways to encourage and support each person to meet the responsibilities of the covenant. This is not a time for judgment.
- Remember that some children may not have acts to report in every area every week. Extend grace, and then encourage children to include acts in all four areas regularly.
- If any of the children have added a personal clause to the covenant, make sure you have written it down. If the child does not mention his or her clause, it is okay to ask about it.

- Use follow-up questions to help children share more fully how they have lived out their covenant during the week.
  - Tell us about the scripture passage you read.
  - What did you learn about God or about God's people?
  - What questions do you have about the passage?
  - What kinds of prayers are you using?
  - What was the best part of worship this week? Why?
  - Why is it hard to be kind to your sibling?
  - Why do you think people are afraid of people who are homeless?
  - I wonder how Mr. Smith felt when you took him flowers from your garden.
- In the beginning, you may need to help children support one another. Some children will take failures quite seriously. Reassure them that God forgives them and expects them to keep trying. Others may not take the covenant seriously enough. Ask questions that will help them think about and articulate what they might do to be faithful to the covenant, such as, "I wonder how our group can help you fulfill this covenant clause?"
- Model and remind children *weekly* to maintain confidentiality. Tell the children that confidentiality is part of building trust in the group so that everyone can feel safe in sharing personal experiences and asking questions without judgment.

Closing Covenant Sharing

After sharing ways the group has followed the covenant clauses, end Covenant Sharing by reading the covenant conclusion together and joining in a time of prayer. Possible approaches to closing prayers:

- At first you may need to say the prayer, but after the group has been meeting awhile, invite the children to offer sentence prayers or to take turns leading the closing prayer. All children will not feel comfortable leading prayer. Do not push.
- Create a group prayer to use each week using the acronym ACTS: adoration, confession, thanksgiving, and supplication (meaning "requests").

- Learn and pray one-sentence prayers that are easily memorized, such as "Make me to know your ways, O LORD; teach me your paths" (Ps. 25:4); or "Create in me a clean heart, O God" (Ps. 51:10); or "This is the day that the LORD has made; let us rejoice and be glad in it" (Ps. 118:24).
- Use a refrain or a hymn round such as "Go Now in Peace" as a sung prayer.

Justice and Compassion Time

The second half of the Covenant Discipleship with Children gathering is Justice and Compassion Time. During this time, children learn about and practice acts of compassion and justice. Justice means being the voice of the voiceless. Through acts of justice, we serve in our world by learning about a justice issue in the community, sharing with others what we have learned about the issue, and taking action to address the issue.

When a part of God's creation (person, animal, or the earth) is not being treated fairly and not being treated with love and care, that's a justice issue. A justice issue arises when equal value is not placed on all persons or there is not harmony among people or creation.

Compassion refers to simple kindnesses and loving others. It includes helping friends and family members, visiting older adults who are shut in, and other acts of offering care to others. Acts of compassion are personal actions that usually occur face to face or in relationship with the person in need. While justice is about fairness, compassion is about care.

Choosing a Justice Issue

In the beginning, it is best for the guides and the coordinator to choose the justice issue for the group, telling them your reason for choosing that particular issue. It is important that the issues be relevant to the children and they can easily comprehend and respond in a meaningful way. Think about the justice issues that you have a passion for, an issue your church is already addressing, or an issue that affects children in the community. Some possible justice issues include the following:

caring for God's creation
disability concerns
foster anti-bullying
homelessness
hunger
racism
peace
poverty

Helping Children Choose Their Own Justice Issues

When children have become familiar with the purpose and process for Justice and Compassion Time, encourage them to choose new justice issues. Ask questions and listen to one another. The following three practices can help the process:

- Take a look at what is going on in the world and in the lives of the children. What issues do your children face at school? What issues of unfairness are being reported in the news? Talk with parents and ask, "What justice issue does your child see or experience?"
- Listen to children so that you know what is affecting them. What are they talking about? What are they angry about? What do they have a passion for? Listening and asking these questions can help the group determine a justice issue that everyone can get excited about.
- Listen to what children are not saying. What are the issues they are silently dealing with that may raise a red flag for you as an adult? For example, abuse, neglect, or violence of children in their classroom, poverty or bullying.

Through these three practices are endless possibilities of discovery and learning.

Planning Acts of Justice and Compassion

Once a justice issue has been identified, plan each week's activities and which guide will be responsible for particular ones. Activities will include ways for children to learn about the justice issue, experience the injustice through simulation games or field trips, and ways for the children to respond or lead others to respond. Decide whether the response will be an act of justice or compassion or both. Covenant Discipleship aims for balance, so be intentional about responding equally between acts of justice and acts of compassion.

Here are some suggestions for your planning:

- Research information about current issues.
- Pay attention to justice issues within local neighborhoods and schools and reported through media. Become familiar with the work and resources of social organizations in the local community.
- Identify community agencies and organizations dealing with the particular issue and review their websites.
- Utilize United Methodist connections—district representatives and conference leaders in church and society, health and welfare, or mission and leaders in United Methodist Women or United Methodist Men.
- Contact the annual conference media center and community library for books and multimedia resources about justice issues.
- Check online video sources for short vignettes and videos.
- When using the Internet for research, check several sources to verify the accuracy of the information you find.
- Identify resource materials available through your church and community library.
- Invite resource people to talk with the children (try to avoid lecturers), arrange for field trips, and gather books, simulation games, multimedia resources, and anything else that will be used.
- Prepare biblical reflections, research statistical information that you want to share with the children, discussion questions, and materials for activities.
- Request necessary room setup.
- Gather supplies and equipment.
- If a monetary cost is involved, talk with the coordinator, and then notify leaders of a particular ministry area or parents or both.
- Well in advance, inform parents of the group's plans and obtain permission and emergency contact for an activity away from the church building.

The Story of Covenant Discipleship with Children at Buncombe Street United Methodist Church

Buncombe Street United Methodist Church in Greenville, South Carolina, has been offering Covenant Discipleship with Children for over fifteen years. Led by Gayle Quay, the minister of children, families learn alongside the children and are challenged each week to answer questions about concerns in the community and the world in which we live. They are actively learning and responding to justice issues.

The children's Covenant Discipleship group at Buncombe Street UMC read and talked about John 13:1-17, where Jesus taught the disciples a profound lesson about the importance of serving. Jesus, in response to the disciples arguing about who was the greatest among them, began to wash their feet. This task of foot washing was reserved for the lowliest of menial servants. Jesus used this powerful illustration to reveal the importance of humble service. In verse 17 Jesus says, "Since you know these things, you will be happy if you do them." We experience great joy and are blessed when we serve the Lord by selflessly serving others.

The Covenant Discipleship group visited several community organizations to learn about the poor in their neighborhood and opportunities for service in their community. They then chose three outreach ministries to launch "Families Who Care." Families in the congregation choose one of these mission outreach projects:

- Food pantry. The children learned that the food pantry feeds over sixty families per week. Each family receives one bag of food containing twenty-six food items that feeds a family of four for three days. After some calculations, the group realized that over 1,500 items are distributed every week! Learning that the agency has an ongoing need for food, the children created a list of food items that are needed.
- Adult education program. The children learned that adults who do not have a high school diploma have limited opportunities for success. The children created a list of basic schools supplies (notebooks, notebook paper, pens and pencils) needed for the adult education (GED) program.

- Community center. The children learned that the center provides canned food and bags of rice, beans, and pasta to families. The children created two different ways to creatively provide food for the center:
  - Buy a large quantity of rice, beans, and pasta (fifty pounds is suggested) and sandwich-size plastic bags. Measure out one cup of the dry food and place in one of the bags.
  - Hold a family food drive by either purchasing canned food items or going door to door to collect canned food.

The families purchase the requested supplies or food, repackage materials as needed, and deliver their offering to the community agency. Families celebrate by taking a photo of their ministry outreach and share the picture with the congregation on a church bulletin board. Catherine, a parent, said about the experience, "It has opened their eyes, and their hearts. They seem wiser and it is easier for them to think beyond themselves."

Writing the Covenant

New groups should devote their first several meetings to writing the group's covenant. Begin with the General Rule of Discipleship, which is the starting point for all Covenant Discipleship covenants: "To witness to Jesus Christ in the world, and to follow his teachings through acts of compassion, justice, worship, and devotion, under the guidance of the Holy Spirit" (*The Book of Discipline of The United Methodist Church 2012*, ¶ 1117.2a).

Remind the children that the covenant is a statement of their intentions for living as disciples of Jesus Christ through acts of devotion, worship, compassion, and justice. Their actions as Christian disciples may involve more than they include in a written covenant, but those included in the covenant are actions that the group promises to live out each week.

Start where the children are in their faith development, not where you believe they ought to be. As the children change and grow in their understanding of the Covenant Discipleship process, the covenant will be reviewed and updated as needed, usually at the beginning of each term.

The covenant has three essential parts: a preamble, clauses, and a conclusion. Children may add personal clauses for growing as a Christian disciple in her or his own life.

Covenant Preamble

The preamble states the nature and purpose of the covenant. Ask the group to read the preamble found in the Sample Covenants on pages 91–94. The group may choose to use one of the sample preambles or write their own. To help the group write their own preamble, ask them to complete the following sentences:

- We promise to live as disciples of Jesus Christ by . . .
- We know that . . .
- Through the Holy Spirit, we will . . .
- We want to grow in our relationship with Jesus Christ and others because . . .

Feel free to add other phrases that will help the children focus on the purpose and nature of the covenant. Once you have several sentences, you may arrange or combine the sentences into the preamble statement.

Covenant Clauses

Balance the clauses of the covenant (no more than six to eight) between acts of devotion, worship, compassion, and justice. Set realistic levels of commitment for the group. It is wise to write only one to two clauses under each of the four headings. Children can overextend themselves, especially when they get excited. Help the children set realistic goals for themselves.

- Review the clauses in the Sample Covenants on pages 91–94.
- Provide butcher paper or sheets of paper on which the children can write their ideas, or you may write for them. Make sure everyone can see the paper (or computer screen, if you prefer that option).
- Ask the children to brainstorm possible acts of devotion, worship, compassion, and justice. You may need to suggest possible acts if they get

stuck. It may be helpful to suggest some possible clauses to the group. The group can choose or adapt a particular clause for their covenant.

- As a group, choose one to two ideas under each heading.
  - Remind the children that they need to write the clause as simple and as specific as possible.
  - Remind them that these are acts that everyone in the group is willing and able to do.
  - If the guides have already chosen the first acts of justice and compassion, write these on the group covenant and explain to the children that this is just a starting point. If someone wants to do another act of justice or compassion, the child can write it under his or her personal clauses.
- Encourage children to add their own personal clauses. These are things that the child chooses to do on his or her own. Remember, not every child will want to add a personal clause, nor is it necessary to add a personal clause.

Covenant Conclusion

End the covenant with a statement that reaffirms the nature and purpose of the covenant and emphasizes again the importance of grace in Christian discipleship.

- Review the conclusion in the two sample covenants on pages 91–94.
- The group may choose to use one of the sample conclusions or write their own conclusion by summarizing thoughts that the group listed in writing the preamble.

Invite each child and guide to sign the group covenant committing to following the covenant. Give a copy of the covenant to each member of the group.

Lesson Plan for the First Gathering

Preparation:

Ask guides and parents to let you borrow camping equipment, including lanterns, sleeping bags, tents, suitcases, duffle bags, maps, and other supplies and equipment needed for a journey.

Cut out footprint outlines to place around the room. Decorate the room so that it looks like you are going on a great adventure.

Make index cards with one action on each card: pray, read the Bible, help others, ride a bike, sing in the choir, be a friend, serve as an acolyte, help a stranger, make a card for someone who is sick, speak up when someone is hurting, and so on. Make sure all four types of acts (compassion, justice, worship, devotion) are covered and add some actions that are not acts, like kicking a ball or washing your hands.

The first meeting of the group is a good time to make or hand out the identifier the children will wear each week (T-shirt, bracelet, visor, pin).

Supplies:

- Materials for children to make their own name tags
- Blank index cards or sticky notes
- Cups of water
- Bowls and napkins
- Trail mix ingredients (be sure to take precautions for allergies.)
- Paper, pens or pencils, Bibles, and hymnals for each table
- On paper or marker board, create two lists—"Loving God" and "Loving Neighbor"
- Copies of "Diagram of The General Rule of Discipleship" and "Compassion and Justice—What Is the Difference?" (located in the appendices)
- For each child, on a colored sheet of cardstock write the word *Compassion* on one side and *Justice* on the other side.

Arriving Activities (5–10 minutes)

Ask the guides to welcome the children as they arrive and invite them to make their own name tags. Direct the children to the snack area to create their own trail mix. Spend time talking with the children to not only learn each child's name but also the child's hobbies, interests, and why they chose to become part of a Covenant Discipleship group.

Group Building (10 minutes)

Pass around a stack of blank index cards or sticky notes and ask each person to take several. Once everyone has cards in their hand, ask them to write one fact that they want everyone to know about themselves on each card. Ask each child and guide to share their name and the facts about themselves. If you have a large group, divide into your Covenant Discipleship groups to share.

What It Means to Be a Disciple (15 minutes)

Say to participants:

> We are starting a journey also known as a pilgrimage to learn about and to practice walking in Jesus' footsteps. When we go on a trip, it is important to get to our destination. However, our faith journey or pilgrimage is different. This journey is lifelong and it is important to focus on what we experience along the way.

Ask participants: What does the word *disciple* mean? (It means a follower, part of a group, a learner, and so forth.)

Ask participants: What does it mean to be a disciple of Jesus Christ? (It means to read the Bible, pray, go to church, be a Christian, care about others, follow God's commandments.)

Ask one of the guides to read Matthew 22:37-39, and then say: "Jesus taught us how to be a disciple. He gave us the Great Commandment to love God and to love our neighbor."

Ask participants: As a disciple of Jesus Christ, what does it mean to love God? To love our neighbor? In the following activity you will address their responses to these questions.

What Is a Children's Covenant Discipleship Group? (10 minutes)

Ask everyone to stand up. Then say:

> We have a *vertical* relationship with God. We are to be like Mary sitting at Jesus' feet listening and talking with God. Just as you grow closer to

your family and friends as you spend time with them, you also grow in your love of God when you spend time in devotion and worship.

Ask everyone to stretch out their arms so that their body creates an image of a cross. Then say:

As we love God, we also love each other. Our arms show the *horizontal* relationship we have in loving others. Just like the good Samaritan, we are to love and care for others. To be a disciple of Jesus Christ, we are to do both—love God and love others.

Say to participants:

When we are a disciple of Jesus Christ, we love God through acts of devotion and acts of worship. (Point out several examples of acts of devotion and acts of worship from the children's list of what it means to love God.)
We also love our neighbors through acts of compassion and acts of justice. (Point out several examples of acts of compassion and, if possible, acts of justice from the children's list of what it means to love our neighbor. If the children have not listed an act of justice, you might tell the children how an act of compassion could become an act of justice. For example, if one of the ideas on the list is to be friends with one another, that is an act of compassion, and when they are friends with someone who is different or isn't included in a group, then that is an act of justice.)

Ask everyone to stand on only one leg. As they stand on one leg, ask them to lean to their right. (There will probably be laughter as they try to keep their balance.) Ask the group to sit down again. Say to participants:

Stories of Jesus in the Bible remind us that it is important in our Christian life to balance *being*, loving God, with *doing*, loving others. Jesus had times for prayer alone, community worship and learning, caring and healing individuals, and standing up against unjust persons and systems. There was balance in Jesus' life. As we strive to live like Christ, we too seek that same balance as we walk in Jesus' footsteps.

Hand out "Diagram of The General Rule of Discipleship." Say to participants:

When we are a disciple of Jesus Christ, we balance our lives. When we focus only on loving God or only on loving our neighbor, we tend to get out of balance. Covenant Discipleship helps us to stay in balance loving God and loving our neighbors. Covenant Discipleship helps us learn and grow in our faith as we practice walking in Jesus' footsteps.

Say to participants:

Each Covenant Discipleship gathering will be divided into two parts, Covenant Time and Justice and Compassion Time. During Covenant Time, you will meet in small groups to pray together, read from the Bible, and talk about how you are growing in your relationship with God. During Justice and Compassion Time, you will learn about justice issues that are important in our lives and in our community. You will have opportunities to practice acts of compassion and acts of justice.

Read some of the examples under each of the acts on the handout Diagram of The General Rule of Discipleship.

What Is Covenant Time? (20 minutes)

Ask each Covenant Discipleship group to sit at a table or sit together in a circle. Ask the guides to explain the Covenant Sharing portion of Covenant Time. The guides need to include this information:

- A covenant is an agreement about what each child will do during the week between meetings. The covenant will include acts of devotion, acts of worship, acts of compassion, and acts of justice that the group will practice.
- Encourage the children to think about and share possible acts under each category. Look at "Living the Covenant" and write down the children's ideas on the paper or marker board you prepared.
- The children will not be writing their group covenant today, but they will share ideas about what they may want to include in their covenant.
- When the children write their group covenant, they will decide on one or two acts for each category. The entire group will need to agree and promise to practice each act.

- Each person will also be able to add one or two personal acts to his or her covenant. These are acts that the person agrees to practice by themselves and the group will encourage and support their commitment.
- During the coming week, the children should continue to think about possibilities they would like to include in their group covenant.

Review what it means to be part of a Covenant Discipleship group. Ask: What does it mean to be part of a group?

- They will work together and support one another as they grow to become faithful disciples of Jesus Christ.
- It is place where they can say what they feel and ask questions without having anyone laugh at them or make fun of them.
- Everything they say or do is confidential. That means they can tell their parents or others what they said, but they cannot tell what others said or did. Tell the group that keeping things confidential is one of the covenant agreements they make.
- The purpose of a Covenant Discipleship group is to help one another walk in Jesus' footsteps by loving God and loving our neighbor—becoming disciples who make disciples.

Close Covenant Time with prayer for the children as they grow in their relationships with God and with one another.

- Ask the children to list their prayer requests. You can either encourage each child to write down the requests or create a group list that is e-mailed to the group later.
- Encourage the children to pray for these requests during the coming week.
- After praying together, you might sing "Go Now in Peace."

Interlude

After fifteen minutes, bring the groups back together with music. This is a good time to learn and practice singing some Covenant Discipleship group songs. These might include "Praise Ye the Lord," "I Am a C-H-R-I-S-T-I-A-N," "The B-I-B-L-E," "I've Got the Joy, Joy, Joy," "He's Got the Whole World in His

Hands," "Amazing Grace," "This Little Light of Mine," "Be Still and Know," "This Is the Day," and other songs that express the love of God and neighbor.

What Is Justice and Compassion Time? (20 minutes)

Read Micah 6:8 and say to participants:

> During Covenant Time we learn and practice walking humbly with God. We pray together and talk about how we are growing in our relationship with God. Each week after Covenant Time the groups will come together for Justice and Compassion Time, when we will practice being disciples of Jesus Christ and discover ways to do justice and show compassion. Sometimes, it is difficult to tell the difference between compassion and justice. We are going to play a game to help us think about the difference.

Use the appendix entitled "Compassion and Justice—What Is the Difference?" to help the children begin to distinguish the difference. Make sure each child has a sheet of cardstock with *Compassion* written on one side and *Justice* on the other. As you read one of the acts, ask the children at each table to choose whether the act is an act of compassion or an act of justice. Ask them to hold up the paper showing the word *Compassion* or the word *Justice* for their answer. After all the groups have chosen an answer, tell the children the correct answer. Help the children understand the difference. Do this several times. Afterward, hand out the appendix entitled "Compassion and Justice—What Is the Difference?" to each child.

Say to participants:

> During Justice and Compassion Time we are going to learn about a justice issue and study what the Bible tells us about the justice issue. Then, we will either teach others about the issue, offer an act of compassion in response, or participate in a mission project in the community. We will be servants of Jesus Christ in our community. We will follow in Jesus' footsteps to show compassion and to do justice.

If the guides have already decided on the justice issue and the acts of justice and compassion that the group will be doing, share this information with the group. You might want to pass out a calendar showing Justice and Compassion

Time activity for each week. Consider doing a quick learning activity to introduce the justice issue.

Share possible acts of compassion and acts of justice. Remind the children that they are not deciding on the acts but sharing all kinds of ideas. Ask the children to continue to think during the coming week about possible activities that offer compassion and do justice.

Closing (5 minutes)

Make announcements and send home any information that the children and parents need for the next week's session.

Briefly remind participants of covenant clauses.

Encourage the children to look forward to inspiring, exciting ways to follow in Jesus' footsteps.

Sing one or two more hymns or songs.

Close with a simple prayer requesting God's presence with the children and guides. Ask God to be with the group as they learn and practice loving God and loving neighbors.

Models for Parent-Child Meeting and Adult Guide Training

Model for a Parent and Child Meeting (1 hour)

Coordinator and all guides participate. Remember to provide child care for younger children so that parents and guardians may participate fully.

Preparation

Draw or tape a large Jerusalem cross on the wall or whiteboard.

Prepare sticky notes or index cards with the acts of compassion, justice, worship, and devotion from the cross diagram written on them, one per note or card (see "Diagram of the General Rule of Discipleship" in the appendices).

Plan and provide a light snack.

Let children make name tags.

Meeting Outline

Opening and Introduction

Open with a song, a prayer, and welcome.

As a group, look at the Jerusalem cross (see "Diagram of the General Rule of Discipleship" in the appendices) and share the following points with parents and children:

- The General Rule of Discipleship's balance between the personal and the public, and works of piety and works of mercy
- Examples of balance in life: gymnasts, riding a bicycle, kayaking
- As you look at the cross, see how it illustrates the way loving God compels us to love others as ourselves. The way we live out this love is in service to others.
- Briefly talk about the differences between acts of compassion, justice, worship, and devotion.
- Allow children and parents to work together to place the sticky notes or index cards in the best spot on the cross. Then discuss how participating in each helps keep disciples balanced.

Dismiss the children to participate in an abbreviated Justice and Compassion Time, outlined below, as parents and guardians continue with the information session, also outlined below.

Justice and Compassion Time Experience

Plan a twenty-minute Justice and Compassion Time for the children to participate in on-site.

- Consider an activity that will offer visual impact for the children, allow them to move around, use artistic skills, and work as a group.
- Make sure that only a small fraction of the time is spent with the guide talking and the children listening.
- Use the justice and compassion list (in the section "What Is Covenant Discipleship," on pages 14–16) to stimulate ideas.
- Ask open-ended questions that allow children to offer their thoughts about compassion, justice, worship, and devotion.

Parents' Information Session

Plan a twenty to twenty-five minute information time for the parents. As you plan, provide a comfortable meeting room and make arrangements for child care. Include the following:

- A brief overview of Covenant Discipleship with Children, including the biblical, historical, and theological foundation for Covenant Discipleship.
- Use the appendix entitled "Diagram of the General Rule of Discipleship," which provides examples of acts of compassion, justice, worship, and devotion.
- Share why Covenant Discipleship groups are important. You might ask a adult guide to share why he or she is participating in Covenant Discipleship with Children. If your church or another church currently offers children's Covenant Discipleship groups, invite a parent to share about his or her child's experience.
- Describe what will happen during Covenant Time and Justice and Compassion Time.
- Allow time to thoroughly and intentionally discuss the importance of keeping confidentiality in Covenant Sharing conversations. Children, especially younger children, will struggle with this, so ask parents to support confidentiality with reminders for their children. Assure parents that two Safe Sanctuaries®–trained, nonrelated, noncohabiting adults will be with the children during Covenant Sharing. They will act appropriately if an issue of safety comes up during this time.
- Talk about the partnership between parents and the Covenant Discipleship guides in nurturing children's faith. Emphasize the importance of support and cooperation as they bring their children to the meetings each week and encourage them to keep their covenant commitments. Children's Covenant Discipleship groups require a significant commitment, and participation should be the child's decision rather than the parents'.
- Provide basic information, including the day of the week for the meeting, the time, the location for the meetings, a typical meeting schedule, and if possible, the planned Justice and Compassion Time activities.
- Provide FAQs (frequently asked questions), a registration form or the registration procedure for online registration, and a commitment card for

each participant. Samples are provided in the appendix (pages 79–114) and online at Umcdiscipleship.org/CDChildren. The commitment form has three sections—a commitment by the child, a commitment by the parents, and guides to support the child. Include other forms that are required in your church setting.

- Designate a date by which children and parents must register and return their signed commitment forms to the coordinator.
- Because transportation is always an issue, make every effort to help parents make necessary arrangements for children to arrive and depart on time each week.

Closing

Gather everyone back together.

Teach them the following movements to help them remember the four ACTS. Justice—Hands and Arms Outstretched. Compassion—Hands over Heart. Devotion—Hands in Prayer. Worship—Hands and Arms Stretched Upward.

Ask parents and children to continue their discussions and to pray at home about their participation. Conclude the evening with prayer.

If there are parents who could not attend the informational meeting, arrange a time to talk with them about what was discussed in the informational meeting.

Model for Training Adult Guides of Children's Covenant Discipleship Groups

Provide each adult guide a copy of this resource and encourage them to familiarize themselves with chapters 1–4 to better understand the purpose and possibilities of Covenant Discipleship with Children and how to use the guide to plan Covenant Time and Justice and Compassion Time.

The purposes of the training session include the following:

- To provide ways for guides to get to know one another and to begin to form a cohesive group
- To describe Covenant Discipleship with Children and how this ministry differs from other children's ministry programs and to explore the biblical, historical, and theological foundation of Covenant Discipleship

- To provide an overview of the developmental needs of third through sixth graders
- To describe and identify what happens during Covenant Time and Justice and Compassion Time
- To review and discuss the adult's role in writing the group's covenant
- To discuss guide's responsibilities in leading Covenant Time and Justice and Compassion Time
- To share ways to help children distinguish the difference between acts of compassion and acts of justice
- To share ways to help children choose Justice and Compassion Time Acts
- To plan the logistics of a typical meeting schedule
- To use this guide for resources and suggestions and explore resources available through the local congregation, annual conference, general church, and the community
- To engage in a variety of spiritual practices and discuss the importance of adult guides' personal practice of spiritual disciplines as they mentor children in their faith development.
- To plan the first Covenant Time and Justice and Compassion Time
- To emphasize the importance of following Safe Sanctuaries® guidelines and policies

Training Session (3 hours with a break)

Room setup:

Hang pictures of older-elementary-age children around the room

Chairs around tables

Use tape to make a large cross on the floor or on a wall, and label it to match the Jerusalem cross on page 87.

On the tables, place copies of information, logos, photos, including the following:

- News stories of justice issues and responses
- Literature from community agencies
- Literature from general church agencies and committees
- Discipleship Ministries of The United Methodist Church

- United Methodist Children's Fund for Christian Mission
- United Methodist General Board of Global Ministries
- United Methodist Committee on Relief (UMCOR)
- Heifer Project International
- Bread for the World
- The Society of St. Andrew
- Justice and Compassion Time resources
- Books
- Paper and pens for note taking
- A highlighter for each participant
- Healthy energy snacks, including dark chocolate

Supplies needed:

Bibles (encourage participants to use them frequently during the session)

The United Methodist Hymnal

Projection equipment for *Disciples Making Disciples* video (optional)

Sticky notes

White board, flip chart, markers, pens, masking or painter's tape

Index cards with "Yes" on one side and "No" on the other; one per participant.

Bookmark the following scripture passages for participants to share:

- Genesis 9:8-17 (covenant with Noah)
- Exodus 19:3-6 (covenant with Moses)
- Deuteronomy 6:1-9 (the Shema)

Make copies of these handouts. These are listed in the order they will be used in the training. Distribute them as indicated in the training module.

- Diagram of The General Rule of Discipleship
- Tips for Writing the Covenant and Sample group covenants (online at umcdiscipleship.org/CDChildren)
- *The United Methodist Rule of Life* (umcdiscipleship.org/CDChildren)
- Covenant Form (see appendices)
- "Compassion and Justice—What Is the Difference?" (see appendices)
- Covenant Discipleship Planning Guide (see appendices)

- "Faith Development: 8–9 Years, 9–10 Years, and 10–11 Years" in *What Every Child Should Experience: A Guide for Leaders and Teachers in United Methodist Congregations* by Melanie C. Gordon, downloadable PDF at http://www.umcdiscipleship.org/resources/what-every-child-should-experience

Opening Prayer

Covenant Prayer (from the Methodist Church in Britain)

> I am no longer my own but yours.
> Put me to what you will, rank me with whom you will;
> put me to doing, put me to suffering;
> let me be employed for you, or laid aside for you,
> exalted for you, or brought low for you;
> let me be full,
> let me be empty,
> let me have all things,
> let me have nothing:
> I freely and wholeheartedly yield all things
> to your pleasure and disposal.
> And now, glorious and blessed God,
> Father, Son and Holy Spirit,
> you are mine and I am yours. So be it.
> And the covenant now made on earth, let it be ratified in heaven.

Introductions and Team Building (15 minutes)

1. Ask participants to do the following:

- Find a person in the room that they do not know or do not know well and introduce themselves. They might talk about where they grew up, their family, their profession, their favorite hobbies, and why they are a group guide for Covenant Discipleship with Children.
- Introduce one another to the group.

2. If you know a Covenant Discipleship coordinator or guide from another church, ask that guide to briefly share how their congregation has witnessed

children growing in discipleship. Consider inviting a child or parent to share his or her experiences. If you are new to Covenant Discipleship, explore additional resources at umcdiscipleship.org/CDChildren.

What Is Covenant Discipleship with Children? (45 minutes)

BIBLICAL FOUNDATION (15–20 MINUTES)

Covenant versus Contract

Ask and discuss as a group:

- What is the difference between a covenant and a contract?
    - Contract—an agreement between two or more parties that is legally binding. If someone violates a contract, then it is broken and becomes null and void.
    - Covenant—an agreement between two or more parties that is binding and also the way that God communicates with us. It is a promise we make. Everyone agrees to keep the covenant even if someone violates it.

Ask three participants to read the following passages from their Bibles: Genesis 9:8-17 (covenant with Noah); Exodus 19:3-6 (covenant with Moses); Deuteronomy 6:1-9 (the Shema)

- Ask: Do these covenants hold meaning for us today?

    Read Matthew 22:34-40, the Great Commandment, to participants. Ask participants to discuss connections between the covenants of the Old Testament and the Great Commandment.

    Ask participants to use sticky notes to brainstorm ways we love God and ways we love our neighbors, and then place them in the appropriate places on the cross. Briefly discuss. You will come back to this *later in the session.*

    Read Luke 10:30-37, the parable of the good Samaritan, to participants. Then ask participants to answer each question yes or no by holding up their index cards to indicate the answer, then ask the participants to share why they chose yes or no.
- Since the road between Jerusalem and Jericho was the most dangerous road in Judea and robbers often posed as wounded people, do you think

that there is a good chance that the wounded man was "playing dead" in order to trap the priest and Levite?

- Do you think the priest and Levite were justified in passing by on the other side of the road, particularly if they were in a rush to get to their religious duties and touching a dead person would make them unclean for several days?
- Do you think that Jesus intentionally told the story with the Samaritan as the hero?

    Write these three questions on chart paper or a whiteboard. Ask participants to share their answers with one or two people:

- Why do you think the Samaritan stopped when the others "passed by on the other side"?
- After reading this parable, who would you say is our neighbor?
- What acts of compassion and justice are illustrated in this story? Take a moment to write these on the sticky notes and add them to the appropriate places on the Jerusalem cross.

    Ask a participant to read Luke 10.38-42, Jesus visits Mary and Martha. As a group, discuss the following:

- How are you like Mary? How are you like Martha?
- What personal spiritual practices help you to listen at Jesus' feet? Take a moment to write these on the sticky notes and add to the appropriate places on the Jerusalem cross.

Share the following with participants:

The Great Commandment is the biblical foundation for Covenant Discipleship. Jesus teaches that we are to love God and to love others. The covenant that each group writes describes how they will love God through acts of devotion and acts of worship and how they will love others through acts of compassion and acts of justice.

HISTORICAL AND THEOLOGICAL FOUNDATION (15 MINUTES)

Write the "General Rules of Our Methodist Societies" on chart paper or a whiteboard and the following phrases below the heading:

First, by doing no harm
Secondly, by doing good
Thirdly, by attending upon all the ordinances of God

Hand out copies of *The Shape of Discipleship* (appendix) and copies of *The United Methodist Rule of Life* (umcdiscipleship.org/CDChildren). Show the presentation *The United Methodist Way* (umcdiscipleship.org/CDChildren). Following the presentation, lead a lighthearted discussion on what these rules look like for disciples of Jesus Christ in the twenty-first century.

As a group, stand around the Jerusalem cross. Say to participants:

The General Rules offer a balance between the personal and the public discipleship. We cannot separate personal holiness (compassion and devotion) from social holiness (justice and worship), and we need the help of intentional community to help maintain that balance. Think about a gymnast on the balance beam. Every step, every flip, and every dismount requires the use of balance. Or consider the person in a kayak. He needs both ends of the paddle to stay upright in the rough waters. As you look at the cross, see how it illustrates the way loving God compels us to love others as ourselves, and the way we live out this love is by service to others.

Discuss as a group ways that older-elementary children live out their love of God through compassion, justice, worship, and devotion.

Worship Together (2 minutes)

Sing a hymn or a familiar children's song that will likely be sung with the children during the Covenant Discipleship gathering. You may need to teach the song first. These might include "Praise Ye the Lord," "I am a C-H-R-I-S-T-I-A-N," "The B-I-B-L-E," "I've Got the Joy, Joy, Joy," "He's Got the Whole World in His Hands," "Amazing Grace," "This Little Light of Mine," "Be Still and Know," "This is the Day."

Break (10 minutes)

Provide a healthy snack to model a typical snack for a Covenant Discipleship gathering.

The Covenant (30 minutes)

UNDERSTANDING CHILDREN OF THE COVENANT

Say to participants:

> Look around the room at the pictures of children. Think of all the children you know in this age group. Share with us some characteristics of children in this age group.

> Next, look at the relational areas of *What Every Child Should Experience: A Guide for Leaders and Teachers in United Methodist Congregations* by Melanie C. Gordon (available at umcdiscipleship.org) and form questions for group discussion. Ask participants to take a few moments to identify where they find the connections to compassion, justice, worship, and devotion, and then invite them to share their responses with the group.

WRITING THE COVENANT

(You will need "Tips for Writing the Covenant," "Sample Group Covenants," and "Covenant Form.")

Say to participants:

> In the beginning, the adult guides are responsible for helping the children write their group covenant. It will take up to three sessions, so be patient. Allow everyone in the group the opportunity to contribute and respond. Talk through each part of the covenant with the children, taking time to define and give examples of each of the areas. Since most children are visual, use the Jerusalem cross as your guide, like we have during this training. Take extra time with acts of compassion and justice, because these can be difficult to distinguish for children.

> Set realistic levels of commitment for the group. Children can overextend themselves when they get excited. Help them set realistic goals for themselves.

Say to participants:

> Let's talk about your needs or concerns in leading the children in writing the group covenant.

LEADING COVENANT TIME

(You will need the appendix entitled "Covenant Discipleship Planning Guide.")
Say to participants:

Covenant Time begins with everyone gathered for prayer and music and reviewing the flow of the time together. If there is more than one group, then the Covenant Discipleship groups dismiss to their meeting spaces to continue the sharing portion of Covenant Time (Covenant Sharing). Do your best to make the transition flow quickly and smoothly.

Once the covenant is written, guides facilitate discussions about the ways that the group has lived into the covenant personally and support one another as disciples of Jesus Christ.

Remind guides that they have a key responsibility to follow the covenant in their own lives and to model how to offer forgiveness and grace when commitments are unmet. They are also responsible for encouraging and supporting each person to meet the responsibilities of the covenant. Say:

Here are some things to remember in leading the Covenant Sharing conversations:

- Remember that some children may not have acts to report in every area every week. Continue to encourage the children to include acts in all four areas regularly.
- In the beginning, you may need to help children support one another. Some children will take "failures" quite seriously. They will need to be reassured that God forgives them. God wants them to keep trying, and the group will continue to support them.
- Others may not take the covenant seriously enough. Ask questions that will help them think about and articulate what they might do to be faithful to the covenant.
- Model confidentiality and continue to remind children to maintain it. Tell the children that confidentiality is part of building trust in the group so that everyone will feel safe in sharing their personal experiences and asking questions.

Leading Justice and Compassion Time (15 minutes)

"Compassion and Justice—What Is the Difference?" (see appendices)

The second half of each meeting of children's Covenant Discipleship groups is Justice and Compassion Time. During this time, children learn about and practice acts of compassion and acts of justice. Say to participants:

> Fairness is a concept that children understand well. Do not be surprised if you have to point out the differences between compassion and justice on a regular basis. It can be a difficult concept. Generally, you may describe compassion as showing kindness for another person. Justice is an action that creates a change that makes things fairer in our community or world.
>
> As children learn about justice issues and respond to these situations, you can help them understand and make connections that distinguish the difference between compassion and justice.

Let's take a look at our Jerusalem cross and point out why certain acts are considered either acts of compassion or justice.

Say to participants:

> In the beginning, it is best for the guides to choose the justice issue for the group, telling the children your reason for choosing that particular issue. As children experience and become familiar with the Covenant Discipleship process, allow them to offer justice issues on their own and work to include them if it is feasible and agreed upon by the group. If it is not, encourage the child to find ways to address it individually.

Use the "Compassion and Justice—What Is the Difference?" handout (see appendices) to brainstorm possible acts of compassion and acts of justice that can be addressed in your community and by individuals in daily life.

- What activities will help the children learn about a justice issue?
- What activities will help them understand compassion?

After ten minutes, invite participants to share their ideas with the larger group. Begin discussing which justice issue the children will focus on first. This should be something that will clearly help children understand a particular justice issue in the community. Plan for an act of compassion that can be completed easily in one of the first two sessions. Remind them to balance Justice and Compassion Time between acts of compassion and acts of justice. Say to participants:

> When you plan the group's Justice and Compassion Time, you will need to decide which ideas your group will use and then plan specific learning activities related to those.

Planning Group Gatherings (20 minutes)

Say to participants:

> Let's look at the Covenant Discipleship Planning Guide (see appendices). Review these points to remember in leading a Covenant Discipleship group:

- Stay updated on additional Covenant Discipleship ideas and resources at http://www.umcdiscipleship.org/CDChildren and those included in this guide (see page 115).
- Think about how you will insure that the children will be able to talk freely and confidentially about important issues.
- Remember that it may take two to three weeks to explain and create a group covenant, especially with a new Covenant Discipleship group.
- Have age-appropriate Bibles available for each child.

NAMING THE COVENANT DISCIPLESHIP WITH CHILDREN MINISTRY

You may want to spend some time naming the Covenant Discipleship group. Some congregations will choose Covenant Discipleship with Children. Names like Prayer Friends Forever (PFF), Sprouts, and Holy Club have been used in some congregations. Choose an identifier that will be recognized by the congregation and the community.

Teach them the following movements to help them remember the four ACTS. Justice—Hands and Arms Outstretched. Compassion—Hands over Heart. Devotion—Hands in Prayer. Worship—Hands and Arms Stretched Upward.

Evaluation (5 minutes)

Ask participants:
> What went well?
> What did you learn?
> What do you still need?
> How can training be improved?

Closing Prayer (1 minute)

Covenant Prayer
Open my eyes to your presence, O God,
> that I may see the sorrows and joys of your creatures.
Open my ears to your will, O God,
> that I may have the strength to keep this covenant.
Open my heart and my hands in mercy, O God,
> that I may receive mercy when I fail. Amen.

APPENDICES

FREQUENTLY ASKED QUESTIONS ABOUT COVENANT DISCIPLESHIP WITH CHILDREN

If I am a member of a sports team, dance or gymnastic troupe, Scout troop, or another group, can I still participate?

You have to decide whether the sport or activity will allow your child to keep the group's covenant to attend weekly, missing no more than one time a month. Making choices is sometimes difficult and every family needs to decide.

Why can't I just come when I can, like with Sunday school or another children's ministry?

Covenant Discipleship is a unique ministry. Since the children build trust within a confidential Covenant Discipleship group, are faithful to a covenant each week, and the Justice and Compassion Time experiences usually develop from one week to another, this is a ministry where you need to agree to come each week rather than to come when you can.

Can I bring a friend to one of the group's activities?

Since Covenant Discipleship is a specialized ministry for those who make a commitment, we ask that you do not bring a friend. Please feel free to invite your friend(s) to consider registering and becoming part of Covenant Discipleship the next time.

As a parent, if my child is not happy in their small group, what can I do?

Encourage your child to meet new friends and explain that Covenant Discipleship is about new experiences, new friends, and doing for others.

How are discipline matters handled?

Discipline issues are handled according to church policy. However, when a discipline issue occurs at a project site, parents will be notified immediately, as it will not be tolerated. The coordinator will work with the parent and child on a plan for future weeks.

Should Covenant Discipleship with Children be something I "make" my child participate because I think he or she should?

You should encourage and offer your child the opportunity. However, since this is a commitment to attend the weekly session as well as live out the group's covenant during the week, the child should feel called to this ministry. Not every older elementary child is ready for this. We are looking for children who have a heart to grow in their love of God and others.

Do I have to wear my identifier (T-shirts, cross, bracelet) to every Covenant Discipleship meeting and every time I serve?

Yes, because it helps participants feel a part of the group. It also helps them to be recognized as part of the group, keeping them safe when they are serving in worship or in the community. Identifiers are worn when groups practice acts of justice in the community.

COVENANT DISCIPLESHIP PLANNING GUIDE

The sample below illustrates how you might use this form to plan Covenant Discipleship gatherings. A blank worksheet follows the sample.

Sample

Covenant Discipleship Planning Guide		
Facilitators:		
Setup, Supplies, Resources:		
Activity	Time	Content
Gathering Time	10 minutes	Provide a healthy snack and time to chat with friends
Gathering Time Snack:		Person Responsible:

Covenant Time		
Opening	45 minutes	Guide calls group together with a rhythmic clap or song
		Guide welcomes children
		Guide offers an opening prayer
Covenant Sharing		Guides and children sing two songs
		Guide outlines the evening
		Break into Covenant Discipleship groups
		Group reads their covenant preamble
		Group shares acts of worship, devotion, compassion, and justice
		Guide reads the selected scripture and group discusses
		Guide introduces the justice activity for that day and how it connects with the scripture
Transition		
Justice and Compassion Time		
Justice and Compassion Time	45–60 minutes	This time is spent *going out into the community* to work for justice or to offer compassion or doing an interactive activity on a justice issue.
Dismissal with Prayer and Blessing	3 minutes	Group reads Covenant Prayer

Worksheet

Covenant Discipleship Planning Guide		
Facilitators:		
Setup, Supplies, Resources:		
Activity	**Time**	**Content**
Gathering Time	10 minutes	Snack and Chat
Gathering Time Snack:		Person Responsible:
Covenant Time		
Covenant Time	45 minutes	
		Covenant Sharing Group

Transition		
Justice and Compassion Time		
Justice and Compassion Time	45–60 minutes	Person Responsible: Activity Details:
Dismissal with Prayer and Blessing	3 minutes	Covenant Prayer

DIAGRAM OF THE GENERAL RULE OF DISCIPLESHIP

The General Rule of Discipleship

To witness to Jesus Christ in the world and to follow his teachings through acts of compassion, justice, worship, and devotion under the guidance of the Holy Spirit.

—*The Book of Discipline of The United Methodist Church 2012*, ¶ 1117.2a

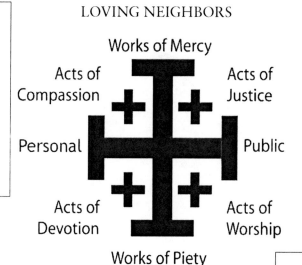

LOVING NEIGHBORS

Works of Mercy

Acts of Compassion

Acts of Justice

Personal

Public

Acts of Devotion

Acts of Worship

Works of Piety

LOVING GOD

COMPASSION
Be a friend to a new student at school.
Help someone without being asked.
Write to someone who is sick.
Give money to a mission.

JUSTICE
Learn about homeless-ness, and then teach others.
E-mail members of Congress about justice issues.
Organize an antibullying campaign.

DEVOTION
Read my Bible.
Pray for Covenant Discipleship group members.
Pray for others.
Journal my questions for God.

WORSHIP
Participate in worship.
Lead worship.
Tithe.
Participate in the sacraments.
Create a devotional.

LIVING OUT OUR COVENANT

Use this worksheet during training and helping children plan out their Acts.

Weekly: _____

Acts of Compassion

LOVING NEIGHBORS

Acts of Justice

_____
_____
_____
_____
_____
_____

Works of Mercy

Acts of Compassion   Acts of Justice

Personal   Public

Acts of Devotion   Acts of Worship

Works of Piety

_____
_____
_____
_____
_____
_____

Acts of Devotion

LOVING GOD

Acts of Worship

_____
_____
_____
_____
_____

_____
_____
_____
_____
_____

Prayer Concerns and Bible Passage Questions

_____
_____
_____

SAMPLE COVENANTS

Sample Covenant 1 for
Children's Covenant Discipleship Groups

Preamble

We want to love God and our neighbors. We want to witness to Jesus Christ in the world through acts of devotion, worship, compassion, and justice guided by the Holy Spirit. We promise these things to God. We know that God will forgive us when we make a mistake, but we will be faithful followers of Jesus Christ.

Acts of Devotion

Read my Bible each week.

Pray for my family, my friends, others in my Covenant Discipleship group, and myself.

Acts of Worship

Attend worship each week.

As a group, learn about the Christian Year.

Acts of Compassion

Write, call, or Skype a grandparent or another family member or friend.

Visit older adults in long-term care facilities.

Acts of Justice

Learn about caring for God's creation and organize a recycling project.

Learn about homelessness and eat lunch and visit with guests at a homeless shelter.

Personal Commitments

(Invite children to write their own personal clauses.)

Covenant Conclusion

We promise to follow this covenant, trusting in God's grace to help us love God and our neighbor in all that we do.

I will be a faithful member of my group as we encourage and support each other.

_____   _____   _____

_____   _____   _____

Signatures of group members

Sample Covenant 2 for Children's Covenant Discipleship Groups

Preamble

We promise to live as disciples of Jesus Christ by loving God and loving others. We will learn to show our devotion and worship to God and we will be kind and just to others. Through the Holy Spirit, we will forgive ourselves and one another when we make mistakes. We will encourage one another as we grow as faithful followers of Jesus Christ.

Acts of Devotion

Read one of the psalms each week.

Keep a list of things I am thankful for each day and offer my prayers of thanksgiving.

Acts of Worship

Serve as an acolyte, usher, or greeter or sing in the choir.

Tithe—give an offering to the church.

Acts of Compassion

Do a chore around the house without being asked.

Send a note to someone who is sad, hurting, sick, or lonely.

Acts of Justice

Learn about bullying and start an antibullying campaign at school.

Learn about hunger and hold a church-wide food drive for the food bank.

Personal Commitments

(Invite children to write their own personal clauses.)

Covenant Conclusion

We promise to follow this covenant, trusting in God's grace to help us love God and our neighbor in all that we do.

I will be a faithful member of my group as we encourage and support each other.

_____   _____   _____

_____   _____   _____

Signatures of group members

COVENANT FORM

Preamble

Acts of Devotion

Acts of Worship

Acts of Compassion

Acts of Justice

Personal Commitments
(Invite children to write their own personal clauses.)

Covenant Conclusion

I will be a faithful member of my group as we encourage and support each other.

_____   _____   _____

_____   _____   _____

Signatures of group members

COMPASSION AND JUSTICE— WHAT IS THE DIFFERENCE?

As Christians, we are called to do acts of compassion and acts of justice, but sometimes it is difficult to distinguish between them. Compassion is showing kindness for another person. Justice is an action that creates a change that makes things fairer in our community or world.

Acts of Compassion	Acts of Justice
Befriend someone who is being bullied. *Your idea:*	Start an anti-bullying campaign at your school or in your community. *Your idea:*
Serve meals in a feeding ministry. *Your idea:*	Simulate a hunger experience, then raise funds and participate in a CROP Hunger Walk. *Your idea:*
Clean out weeds or plant flowers at the church or an older member's house. *Your idea:*	Learn about earth care. Create a ministry that leads the congregation to recycle, reuse, and reduce. *Your idea:*

Pack lunches for the homeless. *Your idea:*	Learn how your community is addressing homelessness and educate your congregation. Explore how you or your congregation will assist in alleviating homelessness. *Your idea:*
Visit an animal shelter and help care for the animals. *Your idea:*	Learn about the humane treatment of animals. Work with church staff to offer a Blessing of the Animals service, and include a time to share what you discovered. *Your idea:*
Befriend someone who comes from a different culture. *Your idea:*	Write a letter to your congressperson about an issue of discrimination. *Your idea:*
Tell a responsible adult if you know someone is being abused. *Your idea:*	Participate in a walk that brings attention to the abuse of children. *Your idea:*

COMMITMENT CARD

Disciple, Parent, Guide,

After you have discussed your participation in Covenant Discipleship with your parent(s) or guardian(s), and you make the decision to commit to membership in the group, please sign this commitment card. Your parents or guardians and your guide will also sign as a promise to support you as a disciple who makes disciples of Jesus Christ.

_____   _____   _____

_____   _____   _____

_____   _____   _____

(*signatures*)

Cut here and keep the information as a reminder.

Covenant Discipleship group will meet on _____ (*day of week*) at _____ (*time*)

From _____ (*beginning date*) to _____ (*ending date*)

REGISTRATION FORM

Child's name _____

Child's age _____ Date of birth _____

Parent or guardian's name _____

Address _____

City _____ State _____ Zip code _____

E-mail address _____

Cell phone number(s) _____

Home phone_____ Work phone _____

Emergency contact name _____ Relationship _____

Telephone number _____

Emergency contact name _____ Relationship _____

Telephone number _____

Special instruction or information listed by parent or guardian: _____

_____

I am the parent or guardian of the above listed child participant and grant permission for him or her to participate fully in the event. I do hereby give permission to take him or her to a doctor or hospital for any necessary medical treatment. I do hereby release from any liability _____ United Methodist Church and any and all adult sponsors, church officers, staff and volunteers in the event of an accident en route, during and/or returning from the event.

You consent that any photos or video or sound recordings of your child's activities or works from participating in _____ United Methodist Church activities are the sole property of the church and may be used by us for any legal purpose without payment to you. Such uses may involve the inclusion of such photos or video or sound recordings in any materials (including our website, publications, promotions, advertisements, or other materials), whether as originally taken or as modified by us.

Parent or guardian's signature _____ Date _____

Printed name _____

REGISTRATION PROCEDURE

Registration begins _____. All registration forms can be downloaded from the church's website at _____.

Procedure:

- Read about Covenant Discipleship with Children on the church website.
- Download and read "Frequently Asked Questions."
- Talk and pray with your child to be sure he or she feels called to be a member of a Covenant Discipleship group.
- Sign the commitment card with both the child's and a parent's or guardian's signature.
- Download and complete the registration form, release of liability, and health form.
- Submit all forms and payment for Justice and Compassion Time supplies fee.

GUIDE EVALUATION

We recommend using an online tool for evaluation to cut down on paper usage and as a convenience for young parents.

I served as:

_____ Guide for Covenant Sharing _____

_____ Guide for Justice and Compassion Time _____

1. What influenced your decision to guide a Covenant Discipleship group?

2. What difference has serving as a guide made in your own spiritual faith and growth?

3. What have you heard the children say about Covenant Discipleship? (no names, please).

4. Describe how you witnessed the Covenant Discipleship group experience influence the lives of children in your group (no names, please).

Rank the following aspects of Covenant Discipleship groups:

	Poor	Fair	Good	Outstanding
Publicity				
Guide Training				
First Session				
Writing the covenant				
Covenant Time				
Justice and Compassion Time				
Journal				
Snack Time				
Closing Session				

Comments:

5. What improvements would you suggest for training guides?

6. What improvements would you suggest for Covenant Time?

7. What improvements would you suggest for Justice and Compassion Time?

8. What issues can you suggest as possibilities for Justice and Compassion Time?

9. What improvements would you suggest for publicity, schedule, preparation, and group configuration?

10. Are you a member of an adult Covenant Discipleship group?

11. Would you be interested in being a member of an adult Covenant Discipleship group?

PARENT EVALUATION

We recommend using an online tool for evaluation. to cut down on paper usage and as a convenience for young parents.

1. Rank the following aspects of Covenant Discipleship groups as you heard about them from your child or experienced them yourself.

	Poor	Fair	Good	Outstanding
Publicity				
Information Session				
Writing the Covenant				
Covenant Time				
Justice and Compassion Time				
Journal				
Snack Time				
Closing Session				

Comments:

2. What has your child said about Covenant Discipleship?

3. How frequently did you have to remind your child to keep his or her covenant? *Often (O); Sometimes (S); Never (N)*

    _____ Acts of devotion (Bible reading, prayer, journaling, and so forth)

    _____ Acts of worship

    _____ Acts of compassion

    _____ Acts of justice

4. What was your child's favorite Justice and Compassion Time experience? Why?

5. If applicable, what kept your child from fulfilling the group covenant?

6. How was the relationship between your child and his or her group guide beneficial?

7. What difference has Covenant Discipleship made in your family life?

    In your child's school life?

    In your child's relationship with friends?

8. What difference has Covenant Discipleship made in your child's understanding of the life of the church?

9. Please complete the sentence: Next time I wish . . .

DISCIPLE EVALUATION

1. Put a check or X in the box that is the best answer for your experience in Covenant Discipleship this year.

	Needs improvement	Okay— I need more practice	Good	Excellent— I learned a lot
Justice Activities				
Compassion Activities				
Sharing in Covenant Time				
Personal Devotion				
Keeping a Journal				
Praying for Others				
Snacks				
Songs				

Comments:

2. What did you learn about yourself during Covenant Discipleship?

3. What acts of justice and compassion do you want to do next year?

4. What would you change about:

   Covenant Time

   Justice Activities

   Compassion Activities

   Personal Devotion

5. What was your favorite activity of the year? Why?

PARENT AND CHILD INFORMATION SESSION: SAMPLE LETTER

Dear _____,

Your child is invited to participate in a unique ministry, Covenant Discipleship with Children, a part of Covenant Discipleship groups of The United Methodist Church. Participants promise "to witness to Jesus Christ in the world and to follow his teachings through acts of compassion, justice, worship, and devotion, under the guidance of the Holy Spirit." Children along with their adult guides will support one another as disciples who make disciples of Jesus Christ by living out the greatest commandment to love God and to love neighbors.

Enclosed you will find a brochure with information regarding the date, time, and location of the Covenant Discipleship group meetings and a list of answers to frequently asked questions. Before making plans to participate, we ask that your child attend a Parent and Child Information session that will be held on _____ at _____ in _____. At the meeting, we will engage in activities that will offer children an experience of Covenant Discipleship and inform parents and guardians about this significant opportunity for children to grow in their faith and discipleship. If you are unable to attend this meeting, we will be happy to discuss Covenant Discipleship with Children with you at your convenience.

Each week as part of the Covenant Discipleship gathering, the children will participate in Covenant Time and Justice and Compassion Time. During Covenant Time, each group of six to eight children and at least two adult guides will offer an account of how they have lived their covenant. The covenant will be written by the group and guides them as they follow Jesus' command to his disciples, "Love the Lord your God with all your heart, and with all your soul, and with all your mind, . . . [and] love your neighbor as yourself" (Matt. 22.37-40).

During Justice and Compassion Time, the groups will gather to learn about and then serve their neighbors in need. Some ways the group might act are educating another small group in the congregation, going out into the community to serve and interact with those who are oppressed, making care boxes for people in need, writing letters to government officials, visiting people who are shut-ins, or organizing a congregation-wide mission project.

The group provides confidentiality, mutual support, and accountability for Christian discipleship. We hope that you will support and encourage your child's attendance each week and his or her desire and efforts to grow in loving God and others. Please make sure that your child has a quiet setting appropriate for Bible study, personal prayer, and journaling as well as an opportunity to take part in family prayer and devotions.

We hope your child will want to be a part of a Covenant Discipleship group! We believe that it is an important step in his or her faith journey. For more information or to register contact: _____.

Grace and Peace,

_____

COVENANT DISCIPLESHIP
WITH CHILDREN

Disciples Making Disciples

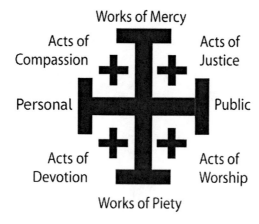

For third through sixth graders who
- want to be faithful followers of Jesus Christ
- want to know how to show love for God and other people
- want to spend time with others who are growing in faith
- are ready to commit time to serving those in need

Jesus gives us the Great Commandment to *"love the Lord your God with all your heart, with all your being, with all your mind, and with all your strength. The second is this, You will love your neighbor as yourself. No other commandment is greater than these."* (Mark 12:30-31, CEB)

Children and adult guides practice
- acts of devotion (listening and relating to God)
- acts of worship (praising God with others)
- acts of compassion (loving others)
- acts of justice (serving in our world)

Join us for an informational meeting:

RESOURCES

An extensive list of resources on Covenant Discipleship is available at http://www.umcdiscipleship.org/CDChildren, including books for children, sample covenants, compassion and justice ideas from Covenant Discipleship groups, pre-confirmation information, writable PDFs, and downloadable logos.

Covenant Discipleship Resources

Accountable Discipleship: Living in God's Household by Steven W. Manskar (Discipleship Resources, 2000).

A Disciple's Journal: A Guide for Daily Prayer, Bible Reading, and Discipleship by Steven Manskar; a new edition of this journal is published each year.

Acts of Compassion

Growing Compassionate Kids: Helping Kids See Beyond Their Backyard by Jan Johnson (Upper Room, 2001). www.upperroom.org.

Acts of Justice

The Children's Fund for Christian Mission. The Children's Fund is a long-standing collaboration between Global Ministries and Discipleship Ministries of The United Methodist Church. The web-based materials provide stories about four children's mission projects around the world and suggested activities for learning about the projects and raising money for the Children's Fund. The materials are available at http://www.umcdiscipleship.org/children.

Acts of Worship

Always in Rehearsal: The Practice of Worship and the Presence of Children by James H. Ritchie Jr. (Discipleship Resources, 2005).

United Methodist Worship Resources: www.umcdiscipleship.org/worship.

Acts of Devotion

Pockets, a magazine for ages six through twelve from the Upper Room. Includes puzzles, games, stories, poems, scripture, and prayers to help children grow closer to God. www.upperroom.org.

Agencies and Organizations

Discipleship Ministries of The United Methodist Church, www.umcdiscipleship.org

United Methodist Women, http://www.unitedmethodistwomen.org/

Disability Ministries Committee of The United Methodist Church. http://www.umdisabilityministries.org/resource.html

Children's Defense Fund, www.childrensdefense.org

Heifer International, www.heifer.org

Institute for Peace and Justice, www.ipj-ppj.org

Society of St. Andrew, www.endhunger.org

United Methodist Committee on Relief (UMCOR), www.umcor.org

COVENANT DISCIPLESHIP
GLOSSARY

---

accountability: Covenant Discipleship groups are accountability groups. They meet weekly for one hour for mutual accountability and support for discipleship guided by the covenant they have written and shaped by the General Rule of Discipleship. Accountability practiced in these groups is simply each member giving an account of what he or she has done, or not done, in light of the group's covenant. It is telling stories about how the group member has lived the Christian life since the last meeting, guided by the group's covenant. The guide, and other group members, can ask questions. The purpose of accountability is to "watch over one another in love" and to help one another grow and mature in holiness of heart and life; loving God with all our heart, soul, and mind, and loving those whom God loves, as God loves them.

acts of compassion: The simple acts of kindness we do for another person. For example, when we meet someone who is hungry, the act of compassion is to give him or her something to eat.

acts of justice: The actions Christians participate in with others, as communities of faith, to address the systemic and institutional causes of our neighbor's suffering. Christ calls us not only to help a person who is suffering, but also to ask why the person is suffering and then to act to address the causes of injustice.

acts of worship: What Christians do together to offer themselves in service to God through praise, prayer, hymn, confession, forgiveness, scripture, proclamation, and sacrament.

acts of devotion: The practices Christians do alone to nurture and participate in their personal relationship with God: daily prayer and Bible reading, centering prayer, keeping a journal, intercessory prayer, devotional reading, writing, and fasting or abstinence.

balanced discipleship: The General Rule of Discipleship helps Covenant Discipleship groups maintain balance between all the teachings of Jesus and mitigates against focusing only on those teachings persons are temperamentally inclined toward. The General Rule helps persons to practice both works of piety (acts of worship and acts of devotion) *and* works of mercy (acts of compassion and acts of justice). It also guides persons to attend to the personal dimensions of discipleship (acts of compassion and acts of devotion) *and* the public (acts of justice and acts of worship). The General Rule of Discipleship is inclusive and practicable.

covenant: Each Covenant Discipleship group writes a covenant shaped by the General Rule of Discipleship. The covenant serves as the agenda for the weekly meeting. It has three essential parts: preamble, a list of up to ten clauses, and a conclusion. The preamble is a shared statement of the group's shared faith in Christ and the purpose of the covenant. The clauses are balanced between acts of compassion, justice, worship, and devotion and appear in the same order in which the practices are named in the General Rule of Discipleship. The conclusion is a brief statement reaffirming the nature of the covenant and group members' shared dependence upon grace to live the Christian life.

General Rule of Discipleship: "To witness to Jesus Christ in the world, and to follow his teachings through acts of compassion, justice, worship, and devotion under the guidance of the Holy Spirit." This General Rule is the foundation of Covenant Discipleship groups. It is derived from the General Rules. Both are found in *The Book of Discipline of The United Methodist Church.*

Jesus' teachings: Jesus summarized his teachings in Matthew 22:37-40: "'You shall love the Lord your God with all your heart, and with all your soul, and with all your mind.' This is the greatest and first commandment. And a second is like it: 'You shall love your neighbor as yourself.' On these two commandments hang all the law and the prophets." The General Rule of

Discipleship and the covenant that each Covenant Discipleship group writes are intended to help Christians obey Jesus' teachings.

weekly meetings: Covenant Discipleship groups meet weekly for one hour. Experience tells us that the weekly meeting is essential. It is the best way for the group to help one another grow in discipleship through accountability and support. Children's Covenant Discipleship groups meet for two to two and a half hours each week to accommodate acts of compassion and justice.

witness: A witness testifies to the truth. A witness has personal experience with a person or event. The experience of witnesses enables them to tell others about the one they know. Christians are baptized, called, and equipped to witness to Jesus Christ in the world. We witness to what Jesus witnessed to: the reign of God that is breaking out in the world and that is coming.

Children's Supplement to the Covenant Discipleship Glossary

Children are quite perceptive and are aware when we juvenilize language. It is our responsibility not to underestimate their abilities while respecting where they are developmentally. Use these terms often in context so that children begin to incorporate them into their own vocabulary. Additional terms can be found at http://www.umcdiscipleship.org/CDChildren

Assurance: Understanding that God is always with us.

Commitment: To be faithful followers of Jesus Christ and to grow in our discipleship

Confirmation: When we will accept Jesus Christ as our Lord and Savior.

General Rules of the Methodist Church: First, do no harm. Do good. Keep to the ordinances of God.

Holy conferencing: Honest conversation with others that encourages us to follow and serve Jesus Christ

Holy living: Practicing acts of compassion, justice, worship, and devotion.

Jesus Christ: Son of God, Messiah, Savior, Emmanuel.

Mercy: Loving neighbor by offering compassion and justice.

Piety: Loving God through devotion and worship.

Pilgrimage: A journey to and through sacred places as an act of religious devotion.

Sacraments: An outward visible sign of inward divine grace. The two sacraments of The United Methodist Church are baptism and the Lord's Supper.

Servanthood: To serve God by offering care and love to others and our world

Social holiness: Christians regularly gathering to care for one another in love and serve God in worship

Stewardship: Caring for creation through gifts and action.

John Wesley's Way of Salvation: God loves us before we even know or accept God's love (prevenient grace). After we accept God's love and grace (justifying grace) we commit to a living like Jesus Christ (sanctifying grace).

Witness: Offering testimony of God's love.

CPSIA information can be obtained
at www.ICGtesting.com
Printed in the USA
FFOW01n1035301116
29748FF